MAGNOLIA

Wiley-Blackwell Studies in Film and Television

Series Editors: Diane Negra and Yvonne Tasker

Experienced media studies teachers know that real breakthroughs in the classroom are often triggered by texts that an austere notion of the canon would disqualify. Unlike other short book series, *Wiley-Blackwell Studies in Film and Television* works from a broad field of prospective film and television programs, selected less for their adherence to definitions of "art" than for their resonance with audiences.

From *Top Hat* to *Hairspray*, from early sitcoms to contemporary forensic dramas, the series encompasses a range of film and television material that reflects diverse genres, forms, styles, and periods. The texts explored here are known and recognized world-wide for their ability to generate discussion and debate about evolving media industries as well as, crucially, representations and conceptualizations of gender, class, citizenship, race, consumerism and capitalism, and other facets of identity and experience. This series is design to communicate these themes clearly and effectively to media studies students at all levels while also introducing ground-breaking scholarship of the very highest caliber. These are the films and shows we really want to watch, the new "teachable canon" of alternative classics that range from silent film to *CSI*.

MAGNOLIA
CHRISTINA LANE

WILEY-BLACKWELL

A John Wiley & Sons, Ltd., Publication

This edition first published 2011
© 2011 Wiley-Blackwell

Wiley-Blackwell is an imprint of John Wiley & Sons, formed by the merger of Wiley's global Scientific, Technical and Medical business with Blackwell Publishing.

Registered Office
John Wiley & Sons Ltd, The Atrium, Southern Gate, Chichester, West Sussex, PO19 8SQ, United Kingdom

Editorial Offices
350 Main Street, Malden, MA 02148-5020, USA
9600 Garsington Road, Oxford, OX4 2DQ, UK
The Atrium, Southern Gate, Chichester, West Sussex, PO19 8SQ, UK

For details of our global editorial offices, for customer services, and for information about how to apply for permission to reuse the copyright material in this book please see our website at www.wiley.com/wiley-blackwell.

Library of Congress Cataloging-in-Publication Data

Lane, Christina.
  Magnolia / Christina Lane.
    p.   cm. – (Wiley-Blackwell studies in film and television)
  Includes bibliographical references and index.
  ISBN 978-1-4051-8462-5 (hardcover : alk. paper) – ISBN 978-1-4051-8461-8 (pbk. : alk. paper)
1. Magnolia (Motion picture)   I. Title.
  PN1997.M2544L36 2011
  791.43′72–dc22

                                                                2010043503

A catalogue record for this book is available from the British Library.

This book is published in the following electronic formats: ePDFs 9781444395259; Wiley Online Library 9781444395273; ePub 9781444395266

Set in 10.5/13pt Minion by SPi Publisher Services, Pondicherry, India
Printed in Malaysia by Ho Printing (M) Sdn Bhd

1   2011

Contents

List of Figures   vi

Acknowledgments   viii

Introduction   1

1 *Magnolia* at the Millennium: Historical
   and Social Contexts   11

2 Through the Viewfinder of a Cinematic "Son":
   Reflexivity, Intertextuality, and "Smart Cinema"   37

3 An Aesthetics of Contradiction: Cinematic Style
   and Televisuality   59

4 Sound and Voice: De-Centering Meaning   79

5 Redemption and Re-Mediation:
   Framing the Deathbed   95

Notes   107

Bibliography   111

Index   115

List of Figures

Perhaps coincidence, Claudia's taxicab crosses paths
with her mother's car in an intersection   5

The hanging of one of the men from Greenberry Hill   12

The pilot who has accidentally killed his blackjack dealer   13

A telestrator diagrams the fall of Sydney Barringer   14

A green light signals that a surprise is coming   16

A frog falls toward Officer Jim Kurring   17

The numbers 8 and 2 are situated in the middle of the phone
number for Frank's Seduce and Destroy program   20

A weather report creates both disruption and continuity   21

During the seemingly inexplicable rain of frogs,
these words insist "but it did happen"   42

Phil explains, "This is that scene"   46

In the final stages of cancer himself, Jason
Robards portrays a terminally ill man   49

Frank T.J. Mackey sells his Seduce and Destroy Program   53

The television is a focal point in *Magnolia*   63

This family photo provides an inaccurate reflection
of Jimmy's family   66

A picture of Earl's lungs   68

An open-ended final shot of Claudia   73

Kurring searches for answers   88

A subjective shot from Dixon's point of view   91

Earl's deathbed   101

Stanley stares at the rain of frogs with wonder   103

Acknowledgments

I would like to thank series editors Diane Negra and Yvonne Tasker for seeing the value in this project, and for providing generous editorial support along the way. They have a tremendous enthusiasm for, and commitment to, this series. I wish to thank Jayne Fargnoli and Margot Morse at Wiley-Blackwell for their keen interest in the film *Magnolia*, and also Janey Fisher and Matthew Baskin for their help in shepherding this manuscript through to publication.

Additionally, I owe a debt of gratitude to my colleagues in the Motion Picture Program at the University of Miami, in particular Bill Rothman, Dia Kontaxis, and Grace Barnes. Their support of my ongoing research and scholarly endeavors has been steadfast. Likewise, the former and current graduate students in the program – among them, Trae DeLellis, Christian Gay, Michael Hable, Michael Laramee, Nicole Richter, Meryl Shriver-Rice, and Funing Tang – continue to both impress and challenge me, helping me to flesh out new ideas that might otherwise have remained dormant.

I appreciate the support, which took various forms, of Vicki Callahan, Michael DeAngelis, Suzanne Leonard, and Linda Mizejewski. Thanks also to Mary Colvin and Stephanie McNulty for their friendship and great humor during the writing of this book, and to Ashley Arostegui and Rebecca Provost, who provided much needed research assistance.

I am indebted to my family – Gretchen Gaines and Saul Weiner, Ken and Deborah Lane, and Hilda and Gaspar González, Sr. – for their constant encouragement and frequent assistance. I am grateful to my son Sebastián, who arrived as this project was developing and showed exceeding patience and good humor during its completion. Finally, I wish to express my love and gratitude to my husband Gaspar González, to whom this book is dedicated. Thankfully, he has boundless resources for thinking and talking about film, history, and culture.

Introduction

When *Magnolia* was released in December 1999, reviewers responded to its brash nerve and presentation of emotional vulnerability. David Denby of the *New Yorker* called it, "a rare case of a great terrible movie" (1999, p. 102). *Sight and Sound*'s Mark Olsen deemed it "a magnificent train wreck of a movie," lauding the "audaciously earnest concoction" (2000, p. 26). In *Rolling Stone*, Mim Udovitch claimed, "*Magnolia* is transparently, almost embarrassingly sincere" (2000, p. 50). *New Statesman*'s Jonathan Romney describes, "You come out of *Magnolia* exhilarated and a little battered, feeling that you've had an authentic blast of the pulse of life" (2000, p. 46). Lynn Hirschberg, in a *New York Times Magazine* article, observed, "[Anderson's] directorial nerve can be both audacious and excruciating – a riveting combination" (1999, p. 52).

In a case such as this, when a film is both criticized and celebrated for its earnestness – its condition deemed by some as "embarrassing" and "excruciating" – the field of film analysis faces both a challenge and an opportunity. It is easier to dismiss or obscure the film's significance than to grapple sincerely with its raw deluge of emotion and spectacle. Diane Sippl suggests that those who find *Magnolia*'s concerns "clichéd" or overwrought are "actively dodging the social gravity, the psychological resonance,

Magnolia, by Christina Lane   © Christina Lane. Published by John Wiley & Sons Ltd

and the emotional poignancy of the conflicts mined in the film's sensitive writing and talented ensemble acting" (2000, p. 4). The film asks us to lower our defenses, take down our guard, and experience emotional and moral susceptibility. At the same time, it obliges and in fact invites critical engagement, creating a space for thoughtful distance and contemplation.

Magnolia appeared on over 80 "Top Ten" lists of films from 1999, garnering praise in the *Los Angeles Times*, *Chicago Sun Times*, *Village Voice*, *Newsweek*, and *Rolling Stone*. It also gained its share of citations as "Worst Movie of the Year." Winning three Academy Award nominations and countless festival awards, the film received particular acclaim within filmmaking circles. Kenneth Turan, for example, remarked that *Magnolia* was "drunk and disorderly on the pure joy of making movies" (1999). Stuart Klawans observed that director Paul Thomas Anderson "follows in the tradition of D.W. Griffith, the first great filmmaker to cut between scenes on the basis of theme and not story" (Klawans, 2000, p. 35). As a movie-lovers' movie, this three hour and eight minute epic appears at first glance to view the medium and histories of film as eternal and transcendent.

Yet, *Magnolia* is undoubtedly a cultural artifact specific to its time of release. As Chapter 1 argues, this work circulated within a broader cycle of 1990s cinema known as "millennial films." *Magnolia* asks American viewers to pause and take stock, before turning themselves over to the twenty-first century. Using multiple techniques such as the director's kinetic style (itself a form of narration), the disembodied narrative voice-over (by Ricky Jay), Aimee Mann's music, and various powerful performances, it poses philosophical and moral questions. Are our lives governed by chaos or cosmic order? In the words of the narrator, do we live at the mercy of chance and things "that just happen" or do unexpected encounters "happen all the time" that allow us to connect, to forge community, to try to change the world? Can we make a difference in each other's lives? The film gradually constructs an ethical position – or a series of ethical positions – that speak to its specific location within broader historical and political contexts.

Magnolia's ethical space is reinforced and elaborated through its layered narrative structure and visual emphasis on multiplicity. Twelve characters within nine storylines come together not necessarily through story and plot but through theme and character conflict. These protagonists, like the film, are bound by place as they encounter "a day in the life" of the San Fernando Valley. The film's name supports a grounding in spatial geography by referencing (and at one point showing) an actual street in the valley, Magnolia Boulevard, to aid in one of several interpretations of the title.

Most of *Magnolia*'s characters have hit a crisis point at the start of the story. Jimmy Gator (Philip Baker Hall), host of the children's game show *What Do Kids Know?*, is confronting his mortality. Having staved off the effects of terminal cancer for as long as possible, he struggles to mask his symptoms during a live broadcast. He has just made a visit to his estranged adult daughter, Claudia, in an attempt to repair their relationship, but she refuses his efforts at reconciliation. Claudia (Melora Walters), meanwhile, comes to terms with an out-of-control cocaine addiction. She spends most of the day holed up in her dimmed apartment while roaming taverns at night in search of escape through anonymous trysts. She will soon meet Jim Kurring (John C. Reilly), a police officer called to her apartment on a noise complaint, whose clean-cut, positive approach to everyday life offers her a ray of hope. Kurring is about to have a very bad day, however, as the well-intentioned cop will lose his gun in a bungled pursuit. He also unknowingly misses an opportunity to solve the case of the day (and potentially retrieve the gun) – a crime that involves his discovery of a murder victim in the apartment of a woman, Marcie (Cleo King). Marcie is participating in a cover-up, though the details of the crime will be left ambiguous.

In another narrative thread, Stanley Spector (Jeremy Blackman) – a 10-year-old contestant on the *What Do Kids Know?* program – is cracking under the pressure of his repeated success on the telecast. Feeling exploited by the entertainment business and underappreciated by his father, Stanley cannot bear to feel "different" anymore. His position is echoed in the character of Donnie Smith (William H. Macy), a former whiz kid who has grown into middle age with nothing but emotional baggage regarding his game show days and his parents' theft of all of his winnings. He has hatched a plan to steal funds from his employer's safe and obtain expensive orthodontic work, in hopes of wooing a male bartender with whom he is obsessed.

In another part of town, former television mogul Earl Partridge (Jason Robards) lies on his deathbed ranting about the mistakes he has made and looking for forgiveness from any direction. His home-care nurse Phil Parma (Phillip Seymour Hoffman), an emotionally sensitive caretaker, attempts to track down the dying patriarch's son. Phil soon discovers that Earl's heir is motivational speaker and infomercial star, Frank T. Mackey (Tom Cruise) – a woman-hating spokesman for an obnoxious men's movement who has changed his real name and rewritten his life story to exclude Earl. As Phil's search for Frank plays out, Frank undergoes a press interview with television reporter Gwenovier (April Grace) in which he slowly realizes that the African American woman knows intimate details of his background. The domineering, manipulative Frank suddenly finds that the tables have turned on him, as his vulnerability is exposed and by a woman of color no less.

As this occurs, Earl's younger, glamorous wife Linda (Julianne Moore) travels from doctor to pharmacy in a state of high anxiety gathering scores of prescription pills. On the verge of a nervous breakdown, she is deciding whether today is the day when she should administer liquid morphine to her husband, thereby facilitating a coma and his eventual death. In doing so, she also grapples with

Perhaps coincidence, Claudia's taxicab crosses paths with her mother's car in an intersection

severe guilt over her marital indiscretions, recognizing in these final days that she deeply loves Earl.

By *Magnolia*'s end, Earl will have passed away, aided by Phil who dispenses the morphine. Frank will have made the difficult decision to travel to his father's bedside and confront his own buried emotional turmoil. Linda will have attempted suicide, ending up in the hospital. (And Frank, whom she despises, will make a compassionate visit.) Jimmy Gator will have died in a freak fire, as he tries to shoot himself. His wife, Rose, will reunite with daughter Claudia after learning that he (more than likely) sexually abused the latter as a child. Kurring will have recovered his gun, after it falls out of the sky. He will also have made a commitment to embark on a romantic relationship with Claudia. She too will decide to initiate a fresh start, presumably leaving drugs behind and endeavoring toward a future with Kurring.

Furthermore, Stanley will have interrupted the live game show broadcast with a public meltdown. By the end of the day, he will for the first time assert to his father, "Dad, you have to be nicer to me." His counterpart, whiz kid Donnie Smith, will have professed his love for the bartender in an embarrassing display. He will also have stolen money, attempted to return it to its rightful place, and fallen off the side of a building, ruining his newly acquired braces. He will have crossed paths with Officer Kurring, who helps him see that he has been unfortunately motivated by false and external values.

Earl's death, Phil's grief, Frank's visit, Linda's rush to the hospital, Gator's bizarre accident, Claudia and Rose's reunion, Stanley's epiphany, and Donnie's encounter with Kurring all take place during a raining flood of frogs. The affective and dramatic buildup of overlapping conflict is answered by a cathartic downpour. The rush of amphibians seems to come from nowhere yet its occurrence follows a firmly embedded emotional logic and is foreshadowed by continual references to the biblical scripture Exodus 8:2 (as I discuss in Chapter 1). In addition to the affective community constructed by *Magnolia*, the characters circulate within a moral and philosophical universe that privileges redemption and transformation. Unlike several corresponding works, such as *Short Cuts* (1993), *Babel* (2000) or *Traffic* (2006), whose character collisions are plot- or event-driven, this film draws its protagonists together into a continually expanding and contracting orbit of affect, melos, and ethical inquiry.

Magnolia has been labeled a "smart film," a category Jeffrey Sconce (2002, p. 349) coined to describe the slick, ironic style of many directors in Anderson's company (e.g., Wes Anderson, Alexander Payne, Todd Solondz). This is partly based on the fact that the filmmaker's preceding *Boogie Nights* (1997) presented an extremely stylized and somewhat detached perspective on its subject matter (the 1970s porn industry). Sconce's essay raises a question about the degree to which *Magnolia* conveys a certain nihilism or at least fatalism, especially given its use of an ironic narrator who ponders matters of fate. It is conceivable, too, to perceive the film as "distanced" and "disengaged" (terms used by Sconce) because it operates, on some level, as a game to be decoded, planting dozens of clues along the way in order to foreshadow its rather shocking, Exodus-style climax. The style appeals to an audience that is highly cinematically literate – and engaged with a hyperactive media universe – by inviting spectators to concentrate on particular details of the mise-en-scène and actively participate in word-of-mouth about the film. Yet the heightened affect and definitive commitment to melodrama encourage character identification as well as a certain emotional engagement or immersion. The film maintains a tension between ironic detachment and passionate investment in a way that suggests the two are not mutually exclusive. As will be discussed in Chapter 2, *Magnolia* is distinctive for the way that it encourages spectators to care deeply about the characters even as we look for narrative clues.

Considering Anderson as a "smart-film" director may be problematic in the long run but it is extraordinarily helpful in situating him within a broader school of rising directors in the 1990s (many of whom have continued to be influential). Wes Anderson, Payne, Solondz, Spike Jonze, David Fincher, and Quentin Tarantino arrived as a new generation trumpeting a distinctive "hip" and reflexive sensibility. With it, they revived and revised 1970s auteur theory, expressing reverence toward that prior decade's auteur-directors while at the same time conveying ambivalence toward those figures and auteurism in general. As one of those younger "mavericks," Anderson pays tribute in his films to such noted American directors as Robert Altman, Sidney Lumet, Jonathan Demme, and Martin Scorsese through imitative references and stylistic re-interpretations.

As this renaissance of new auteurs occurred, many (Anderson included) took up the position of adoring yet ambivalent sons, drawing on the inspiration of the earlier generation of forefathers while seeking to make a break from the past. Given *Magnolia*'s preoccupation with father-son relationships, it metaphorically and symbolically stages this generational divide. The central axis of all of Anderson's films to date (from *Hard Eight* (1996) to *There Will Be Blood* (2008)) turns on the subject of patriarchal legacy, suggesting that they seek to re-write and rearticulate auteur theory even while at times perpetuating a romanticized "cult of the director." *Magnolia* and these other works therefore speak directly to (and reflect) developments in the field of "masculinity studies," which emerged in the early 1990s. Anderson's career burgeoned at the same time that these new critical paradigms impacted cultural and film studies. A meta-cinematic text, *Magnolia* takes into account the contribution of contemporary academic gender studies as well as interventions in traditional auteur theory. Its complex cinematic style, discussed in Chapter 3, is driven by multiplicity and contradiction, ultimately posing questions about basic formulations within film and media studies.

In deliberating on the subject of Anderson's directorial role, the tension between his self-effacement and self-insertion becomes clear. In some ways, deep pockets of space are created for characters to exercise their own voice – that is, for multiple and contradictory centers of ideological and thematic gravity. *Magnolia* is structured by what John Bruns labels "polyphony," meaning that it allows for multiple and autonomous voices. Aimee Mann's music, addressed in Chapter 4, served as an origin text for the screenplay and then evolved as the story became more concrete. Mann's presence implies authorial collaboration and results in a multi-vocal structure (this is supported by the fact that another source of *Magnolia*'s inspiration, The Beatles' "A Day in the Life," was written by both John Lennon and Paul McCartney (Udovitch, 2000, p. 46)). In addition, the film is disposed to a certain degree of ambiguity, which encourages viewers to construct their own meaning by singling out what *Magnolia* means to them. As it is hard to sum up or categorize, many spectators return for a repeat viewing, or to seek out Internet details and DVD special features, behaviors that have contributed to the film's cult status.[1]

In other ways, however, the intense cinematic style and knowing "winks" to the audience potentially function to privilege the director's voice over all others. Moreover, Anderson has positioned himself as the primary authorial force through extra-cinematic means such as interviews, websites (such as the now defunct cigarettesandcoffee.com) and detailed DVD packaging. These strategies provide evidence of his investment in guiding audience interpretation. A complex tension exists, therefore, between his repeated attempts to control reviewer and audience response and the film's overall resistance against a unified or authoritative point of view.

If *Magnolia* is a meditation on its own millennial context as well as on the legacies of patriarchy, it is also a contemplation of the cinematic medium. Referencing not only this most recent transition into the twenty-first century, the film specifically invokes the turn-into-the-twentieth century moment of the "fin de siècle" by opening with a sequence shot by a 1911 hand-cranked Pathé camera. Chapter 5 will show that *Magnolia* is preoccupied with the origins of motion pictures even as it grasps for a new vocabulary of artistic representation that expands in the direction of multi-media, the Internet, and digital modes such as gaming and mobile communication. A deep respect for film history comes through in the homages paid by the film to the (often trivialized) genres of melodrama and the musical. While cinema does take precedence in many ways, there is a cultivation of numerous related approaches to representation, including theater, photography, animation, opera, and music. The medium given the most primacy, second to celluloid, is television, which acts as a visual prop from scene to scene and determines the look of certain sequences. The "televisual style" (see Chapter 3) creates a dual sense of flow and fragmentation that merely recapitulates *Magnolia*'s numerous ambivalences and equivocations. This film aspires to embody tensions between and within these many technologies – moving pictures, television, digitality – in such a way that its fixation on the subject of redemption conveys an even deeper concern over the death and rebirth of cinema.

Chapter 1

Magnolia at the Millennium
Historical and Social Contexts

Magnolia opens with three stories interlaced into a six-minute vignette. Over a black screen, a male voice-over (by Ricky Jay) launches into narration. He begins by recounting a tale from 1911 set in Greenberry Hill, London. Three men were hanged for robbing and killing a beloved town pharmacist. In a twist of fate – perhaps "only a matter of chance," according to the voice-over – the three men's names were Joseph Green, Stanley Berry, and Daniel Hill (hence, "Greenberry Hill"). The first shot of this sequence, and therefore the entry point of the entire film, shows the hanging of one of the men. He stands on a wooden platform before plunging to his death, with a sack over his head and the number 82 on his prisoner's uniform. Harkening back to its early twentieth-century setting – and the era of silent cinema – *Magnolia* presents this introduction through a viewfinder. Shot by an authentic Pathé camera from that time, the scene simulates the film stock, camera apparatus, and sepia tone of the period. The device of the viewfinder results in a frame-within-a-frame, creating the illusion of 35mm projection. This is "celluloid" – cinema still in its early stage of inception. Yet, its initial images represent death, a lone figure dangling by a rope.

From birth – or, to be specific, from filmic origin story – to death to rebirth. If we give credence to Thierry Kuntzel's claim that every

Magnolia, by Christina Lane   © Christina Lane. Published by John Wiley & Sons Ltd

The hanging of one of the men from Greenberry Hill

film's first few minutes manifest its overall design, then this opening foregrounds themes of mortality and redemption through its formal properties (1980). Endeavoring to revive the medium, *Magnolia* proffers itself as part of a larger rebirth of cinema. The sheer velocity of this opening sequence implies that it represents a resuscitation, an attempt to breathe life into a (potentially) dying form.

As the vignette continues, the narrator relays another strange encounter, a scuba diver who was accidentally dragged by a small (water-carrying) plane during a forest fire. It is June 1983 in Reno, Nevada and the scuba diver, who is also a casino black-jack dealer, has died from the accident. The pilot of the plane, as it turns out, had provoked an altercation with the diver-dealer just the night before, when he had been dealt an unsatisfactory hand at the blackjack table. After the accident, when he is unable to bear the guilt that he has taken the life of this man – a man he had attacked – he commits suicide. This story poses one of

The pilot who has accidentally killed his blackjack dealer

the film's central questions: can individuals forgive themselves for the irrevocable wrongs they have committed? It also presents the first of the film's references to flowers as a metaphor for community. As the shotgun blasts off-screen, the pilot's blood splatters onto a painting of multiple magnolia blossoms.

The final sequence of this prologue depicts a strange series of events set in Los Angeles in 1951. A young man, Sydney Barringer, commits suicide by jumping off the roof of a tall building. During his fall, he is shot by his mother who has pulled the trigger on his father just a few stories below. The bullet misses the father, flies out the window, and lodges itself in Sydney's back. In case these spatial relations are too complex, a digital pen emerges from the non-diegetic sphere to draw a diagram of the action. This pen, which simulates the telestrator, or television illustrator, was famously used by National Football League commentator John Madden to depict game movements during instant replay. A similar reference would later appear in *Pulp Fiction* (1994) when Uma Thurman, accompanying John Travolta to Jack Rabbit Slims, "draws" a rectangle on the screen ("Don't be a square," she says). As in *Pulp Fiction*, this instance interrupts the narrative flow while also referencing the medium of television. The effect of the telestrator in *Magnolia* is to introduce

A telestrator diagrams the fall of Sydney Barringer

visual reflexivity in a way that foregrounds cinema's plasticity – a condition enhanced by digitality. Just as the three preliminary tales suggest, anything can happen, even within the frame. In fact, the transformative, roaming, questioning quality of this opening serves as preparation for the remaining three hours. Its backward-forward momentum and constant querying take the form of provocation: it asks spectators to open their eyes to a new – or at least renewed – way of seeing. We too should be prepared to replay and review events as they unfold.

The film's opening also presents children as exemplars of this renewed perspective. In the Barringer suicide-murder story, Sydney (we are told) had revealed his plans to a neighbor – a young boy – just a few days prior to the incident. This boy acts as a witness, a listener, a knowing subject, and a narrator in his own right, given that he fills in the blanks for the police. He serves much the same role that Stanley Spector, the young game show contestant, will play in the larger story. Marginalized and taken for granted, Stanley not only knows more (intellectually and emotionally) than the surrounding adults; but he also anticipates the film's final "catastrophe" and reacts openly without fear or question. Sippl remarks, *Magnolia*'s "children are the truthseers and soothsayers"

(2000, p. 7). When the frogs rain down and most (adult) characters express fear, Stanley merely shows wonderment as though he has known something like this event would come and that he has in fact been hoping for it.

This prologue comes to a close as the camera pushes in on the boy. The voiceover narration unites with his piercing gaze into the camera, reinforcing the boy's role as a knowing narrator in his own right. It is at this point that the film – through the narrator – poses its governing thesis: "and [the Barringer death] is, in the humble opinion of this narrator, not just 'something that happened.' This cannot just be 'one of those things.' This, please, cannot be that. And for what I would like to say, I can't. This is not just a matter of chance. Ohhh. These strange things happen all the time." This commentary is made all the more significant because it is spoken by Jay (who also appears in the film as television producer Burt Ramsey), a film and television actor even better known as a magician. As a master in the art of sleight of hand, he lends credence to the argument against random chance. Within professional magic, an intentional design exists behind every trick. Cause and effect govern each action. Yet Jay's voiceover is somewhat ironic and over-the-top. His performative style results in an excessive quality, opening up the space that questions the very "order" he proposes. He is in fact both mimicking and mocking the authority associated with typical narration.

Following the logic of the voiceover, *Magnolia* sets out to show that life's chain of events have a greater meaning – a grand design – and that, by extension, each individual's moral choices carry weight within a larger community. The film ultimately revolves around a question of faith – a refusal to believe only in chance. Its own style and structure *feel* as though nothing is left to chance, appearing to have an organic and pre-conceived architecture.

The best example of this notion that *Magnolia* expresses an underlying, independently moving *consciousness* is realized two hours and 42 minutes into the film, with its climactic rain of frogs.

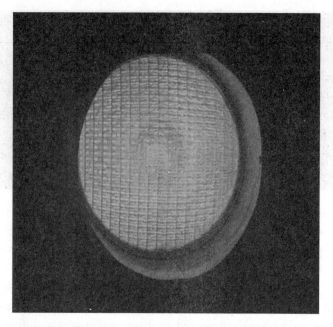

A green light signals that a surprise is coming

Within each story line, various characters have reached a breaking point. Jimmy Gator has just confessed to his wife that he may have molested Claudia, at which point his wife walks out on the marriage. Frank has finally made a visit to Earl (now in a coma) and begins to cry at his bedside, begging him not to die. An ambulance rushes Linda to the hospital. Donnie has been overcome by shame at his crime and returned to the store to put the stolen money back. He sits in his car asking, "What the f**k am I doing?" And Claudia has run out on her date with Jim Kurring after allowing her insecurities to get the better of her.

The sequence begins as Claudia (in a taxicab) and her mother (in a car) unknowingly pass each other at an intersection. The street sign reads "Magnolia," providing an initial cue to start paying attention – a wake-up call to this climactic sequence. The camera

A frog falls toward Officer Jim Kurring

cranes from an extreme long shot of Claudia's vehicle to a close up of Rose, cinematically linking the two women and previewing a more significant meeting between the mother and daughter that will unfold shortly. A cut to a medium close up shot of the traffic signal, as it changes from red to green, announces a shift into cinematic overdrive, so to speak: a cataclysmic event is about to begin.

With this, Jimmy walks toward his kitchen (his daughter's portrait hovering on the wall behind him) and loads a gun. Donnie approaches the store's door only to realize that his plans to rectify his theft have been foiled; the key has broken in the lock. Officer Jim (from his vehicle) spots Donnie scaling the wall of the store. He decides to make a u-turn in order to thwart this would-be intruder. As his car curves around, a frog falls splat on the windshield. And, a second frog lands on the hood. Panicking, Jim swerves and slams on the brakes. As he tries to absorb what is happening, he looks out the window and up at the sky. A subjective shot from his point of view renders several frogs hurling down from the blackened sky, picking up speed before crashing onto his car. A hard, relentless rain of countless frogs ensues, as the sequence moves from character to character, linking them through crisis.

This rather unconventional device manifests an epic-scale catharsis and a moral cleansing for almost all the characters simultaneously. (It appears that Jimmy is the only protagonist not spared from his own self-loathing. He is punished by the film in that he does not finally even have the choice to end his own life. A frog causes his death when its fall results in the gun blasting into the television set, setting off a deadly fire.) By the conclusion, most characters have "weathered the storm" in a way that binds them together, again thematically rather than through narrative conflict. The choice of rain as the overriding experience is appropriate given that *Magnolia* is dripping with affect: tears fall, emotions flow, and, not incidentally, the rain pours. The film's debt to the "weepie" is reinforced by the vertical movement of its direction.

The rain of frogs has received major criticism by those who view it as a *deus ex machina* that erupts out of the blue. Some reviewers perceive it as an external plot contrivance made to compensate for an inability to resolve dramatic conflict through character-driven or narrative-based techniques. *Magnolia*'s defenders point to the fact that the film lays an internal foundation for the event. Anticipatory clues about the frogs, and the related scripture Exodus 8:2, arise frequently. Both are foreshadowed through a repetition of the literal appearance of the term "Exodus 8:2" (or simply 8:2, or random references to 8s and 2s).[1] The book of Exodus in the Bible's Old Testament tells the story of Israel's delivery from Egyptian slavery. In Verse 2 of Chapter 8, God conveys through Moses a command to the Pharaoh to release the slaves, threatening to otherwise plague his country with frogs.[2] This passage informs *Magnolia* because of its emphasis on freedom from oppression and because it communicates a message of redemption and renewal. These characters have hit the point at which they cannot save themselves from themselves. Divine intervention brings a new day.

The visual and narrative cues that set up the rain of frogs are not as noticeable during an initial viewing – as scenes unfold – as they are in retrospect. Therefore, one of *Magnolia*'s distinguishing factors is its manner of inviting audiences to engage in repeat viewings to reconstruct and deconstruct the cinematic ground on which the film is built. Due to the relative subtlety of the signs, the complaint that the final turn of events comes unexpectedly is valid. This is especially true if one expects plot-, story-, or character-driven cause and effect. Yet within the film's emotional and moral terms, the frog flood is motivated. Its dimension of surprise is necessary.

It is important to recognize that the reference to the plague of frogs is not a case of *Magnolia* – or its "creator," Anderson – "finding religion" at the end of the film. This would imply both a last minute emergency ploy to achieve a coherent conclusion for a series of loose ends as well as a problematic attempt to escape the ideological implications and material conditions portrayed by the film. The film is too architecturally sound, on the one hand, and too skeptical about consumerist capitalism and misogyny on the other for this. According to Shane Hipps, "the numerological foreshadowing is largely found in the margins," yet *Magnolia*'s "trick is that the true meaning of the film is [also] found in the margins." He posits that "the frogs falling from the sky are not a random interjection, but rather the only possible conclusion to this story" (2003).

The various appearances of 8:2 are too numerous to document (there are at least 50 of them). The film's opening vignette, previously discussed, offers several examples. In the first story, the hanged convict wears the number 82 on his uniform. In story two, the pilot's plane boasts 82 on its side door. When he plays blackjack, the dealer gives him the cards 8 and 2. In the third story, 82 is spray-painted on the roof's wall just a few feet away from Sydney. His parents' apartment address is also 82, as indicated by their front door. So within the first six minutes, the number surfaces at least five times. In a less obvious instance, the toll-free number listed in Frank Mackey's self-help advertisement is 877-826-3437 (also presented as 877-Tame-Her). The phone number's placement

The numbers 8 and 2 are situated in the middle of the phone number for Frank's Seduce and Destroy program

within a close up of Frank positions the middle "82" within the center of the frame. In a more obvious example, an audience member at the taping of *What Do Kids Know?* holds up a hand-made sign that reads "Exodus 8:2." To conclude with one of the most fleeting instances, just before the frogs start falling, Officer Kurring drives by a banner for a warehouse sale followed by the briefest flash (only a few frames) of a green neon sign with the small letters, "Exodus 8:2."

Further allusions to the pending rain of frogs emerge in the sprinkling of "weather reports" that segment the film. An early interruption occurs 12 minutes in, as a transition occurs between an extended character introduction and the launch of the diegetic action, a scene at the site of a domestic disturbance call for Kurring. Serving a function similar to a DVD chapter stop, the report states, "Partly Cloudy, 82% Chance of Rain." Inserted against a backdrop of blue

Partly Cloudy, 82% Chance of Rain.

A weather report creates both disruption and continuity

skies and intermittent clouds, accompanied by (non-diegetic) musical chimes, this bridging shot lasts 10 seconds. Two more weather announcements appear – the first at 42 minutes and the last at 2 hours 22 minutes. The middle break is more ominous with darker clouds, heavy music, and windy weather on the way. The final one is super-imposed over the Magnolia Boulevard intersection, setting the stage for the frog sequence and announcing that the "rain [is] clearing."

The weather reports work to both halt and advance the film. While they help ground the story in time and place, and also directly address the viewer, they create distancing breaks in the narrative. At the very least, they encourage the viewer to question why the interruptions are there, ushering in moments for pause and reflection and allowing the film to breathe. They also point to an autonomous consciousness that lives both inside and outside the film – an omnipotent presence that is not only capable of forecasting atmospheric conditions but also connecting the dots between the climate and the characters' lives. Is it Anderson, as director, behind this presence or is it a deeper consciousness, over which Anderson both can and cannot exert control? The blueprint of this grand design may elude even the director, *Magnolia* suggests, which speaks to the unknowable and inaccessible aspects of the film. In other words, authorship represents more of a struggle *with* film (or other media) rather than a veritable imprint *on* film (or other media).

"The End of the World as We Know It"

For obvious reasons, the weather forecasts and the rain of frogs contribute to the apocalyptic sensibility of *Magnolia*. These phenomena signal broader themes about "the end of the world" that structure a number of "millennial films" such as *Armageddon* (1998), *End of Days* (1999), *The Perfect Storm* (2000), *The Sum of all Fears* (2002), and *The Day After Tomorrow* (2004). Such blockbusters conjure up potential doomsday scenarios that gesture toward a "final judgment" of contemporary society.

The millennial cycle also includes more existentialist films such as *Traffic* (2000) and *Crash* (2004), which not coincidentally share *Magnolia*'s geographical setting of Los Angeles. *Magnolia* is more closely aligned with these character dramas than the millennial action films; like the dramas, it features an ensemble cast and multiple storylines. *Traffic*, *Crash*, and *Magnolia* each function as a response to and a reflection of American cultural anxieties about the culmination of the twentieth century and the dawn of an unpredictable day. Los Angeles serves as a microcosmic lens through which negotiations of class, gender, and multiculturalism speak to broader conflicts facing the nation. In the case of the gritty, pseudo-documentary *Traffic*, a commentary on North America's losing battle in the war on drugs translates into a critique of US capitalism. With *Crash*, an intense examination of contemporary race relations suggests that everyday personal interactions have become cold and dehumanized. While blockbusters such as *Armageddon* or *End of Days* are obvious instances of the disaster genre, *Magnolia*, *Traffic*, and *Crash* explore psychological and interpersonal "disasters" in their efforts to more fully comprehend the very specific social conditions that define the millennium's historical moment.

Magnolia ponders the millennium by channeling free-floating ideas rooted in the Judeo-Christian tradition that prophesize a "second coming" of the Messiah. These notions, which typically had been relegated to the fringe or paranoid realm, became common currency in the 1990s mainstream, especially on television and in the popular press. Television programming, Hollywood films, and print media drew on dubious yet increasingly referenced allusions to the New Testament's Book of Revelation. Various forms of mass media showed concern that in the "dawn of the third Christian millennium [there] was the slim chance that even one of the world's countless eschatological theories might come true" (Feit, 2004, p. 134). Jonathan Scott Feit posits, "With the approach of the millennial shift, religion took on a tangible sense of foreboding and leapt noticeably to the foreground of the Western collective consciousness. One did not have to be highly religious or a believer in millennial prophecy to worry" (2004, p. 134).

An obvious example of such apprehension within the media occurred in the Y2K (Year 2000) scare: the press reported (and fed) massive fears of a worldwide computer crash, caused by an underdeveloped time coding system that had occurred in the early years of programming.[3] Some despaired that humankind would experience a major downfall in an environment where science was out of control. As Robert Lamm puts it, "Technology promises a paradise on Earth, but Western culture perhaps cannot forget that the original price of wisdom was expulsion from Eden" (1991, p. 7). Had industrialized countries simply gone too far in the search for knowledge and advancement?

For most, however, the Y2K worries were overblown. They were a product of hype that served television and news ratings.

John McCullough explains, "the theme of epochal catastrophe rang through the media and checkout scanners from the White House podium to the West Samoa Hilton (where the 24-hour coverage of New Year's Eve finally wound down)" (2000, p. 54). The absurdist quality of the live news coverage is captured by McCullough as he recounts a CNN anchor's New Year's reportage "that nothing unusual was happening in Times Square but that one should always be aware that L.A. was only three hours away, and crisis could be just around the next ad break" (2000, p. 54). Hour by hour, and city by city, commentators expressed surprise that ordinary life continued as usual, an obvious ploy to keep viewers on the edge of their seat and tuned in until the threat had apparently passed.

Though it is true that many Americans were not overly concerned about Y2K and saw the apparent crisis as media frenzy, a good number of them found reasons to be anxious about more realistic or pressing concerns. This was especially so for those who considered themselves informed or socially conscious. Around the world, numerous hotspots and political conflicts suggested that civil war, aggressive nationalism, and genocide were on the rise. The break-up of Yugoslavia (and the large-scale ethnic cleansing against non-Serbians), genocide wars in Rwanda, and the Battle of Mogadishu in Somalia caused dismay and uneasiness. Intolerance and violence were apparently growing worse rather than better, even as developing countries were purportedly becoming more civilized. In addition, issues of global warming and environmental sustainability began to take center stage, as the planet's ecosystems appeared increasingly over-burdened.

Moreover, the 1990s had been a decade in which the US economy, under President Bill Clinton, underwent the largest sustained expansion in its history. Accelerated capitalism, globalization, and rapid technological innovation placed the country at a distinct advantage worldwide and benefited many wealthy and upper-middle class Americans. Yet such global expansion and the rise of the hi-tech economy caused numerous "unintended consequences" (a phrase first coined earlier in the century by sociologist Robert K. Merton). Domestically, the American class system was being shaped by an increasingly influential professional-managerial class at the same time that the service sector was becoming technologized. The United States saw a serious decline in its manufacturing base and a sudden rise in certain inflated economies related to information technologies, real estate, and finance. Even as excess came to define the decade, many people experienced a loss of real income, a rise in inflation, and other uncertainties due to a series of recessions that dated back to the early 1970s. The successful "bubble markets" that dominated late in the 1990s meant that many members of the working- and middle-classes faced a disparity between the expansionist rhetoric of the American economy and their everyday experience. People's economic lives were becoming increasingly mystified.

In a related trend, the image of the slacker took hold in the 1990s. Downwardly mobile young adults were re-cast as disinterested workers; they were represented as apathetic toward work and adulthood in general. The idea that the emerging generation was simply "slacking" obscured the fact that they faced a declining job market and rising costs of living. Some Generation X-ers chose slackerdom as a form of resistance against financial and economic conditions; others were struggling in their earnest attempts to gain economic footing. However, regardless, the decade became defined as one in which young people were alienated from labor and detached from the proverbial "American Dream."

Internationally, poorer or more underdeveloped nations suffered as richer and more dominant countries succeeded. The surrounding circumstances of the North American Free Trade Agreement (NAFTA) provides a solid example of how globalization intensified disenfranchisement in Mexico – through the development of

Maquiladoras – and decreased manufacturing jobs in the United States at the same time. While globalization may have contributed to America's wealth, it escalated outsourcing and off-shoring of US jobs and created disadvantages for many in the working classes around the world.

Considering all of these factors, it is easy to see why many Americans felt that, by the late nineties, both the nation and the world were at a crisis point. Amid an overall mood of escapism and abundance, underlying tensions percolated. *Magnolia* captures this tension between a superficial sense of material success and deeper questions about existing social conditions. The film translates implicit ideological and political concerns into emotional and ethical ones capitalizing on the fact that melodrama often speaks to the former by mobilizing affect. It posits that social change is possible though it does so through themes of individual transformation. In other words, the outward attention to *characters* – as sites of change – indicates an inner preoccupation with *contexts*. As an example of millennial cinema, *Magnolia* imagines its way through the crisis, looking toward a new way of envisioning existing problems. It searches out a newly invented post-apocalyptic space.

Resisting a closed, predetermined universe, the film constructs an open narrative field almost exclusively "concerned with the possibility of breaking out of confinement" (Sippl, 2000, p. 7). Here again, its complex structure and aesthetic approach support an underlying proposition that everyday choices represent social and often political acts. The rain of frogs, then, symbolizes an "initiation into community" (Sippl, 2000, p. 7). As the characters connect without necessarily even knowing it, we as spectators are encouraged to see ourselves as part of that community. As Sippl puts it, we are "invited to enter its world freely, as critics and aficionados, to take up a position within that world and see it expand. We can grow by helping to create a place that includes us" (2000, p. 7). *Magnolia* levels power relations and emotionally involves viewers, thereby charting a passage out of its underlying narrative – and cultural – conflicts.

This is a path with multiple positions and potentialities that heralds the possibilities of a radical ideological shift. The move is meant to occur both outside (in the characters, in context) and inside (within us). The interplay between the film's outer surfaces and inner emotional layers, shows the heavy influence of the 1950's melodrama. In this genre, high affect often stands in for broader social and political concerns that are not, or cannot be, explicitly articulated. However, *Magnolia* is equally related to Cold-War era science fiction, thriller, and noir films, which mediated apocalyptic themes by staging doomsday scenarios and deeply distorted settings.

The American climate of the 1950s was dominated by the reality of the atomic bomb in the nuclear age as well as increased anxieties related to the Red Scare. *Magnolia*'s existential questioning is quite reminiscent of Cold War, apocalyptic films such as *Panic in the Streets* (1950), *The Day the Earth Stood Still* (1951), *Them!* (1954), *Kiss Me Deadly* (1955), and *Invasion of the Body Snatchers* (1956) which stressed the notion that the country (and the world) had crossed a new threshold from which there was no turning back. A formulation by Sippl not only illustrates the thematic connection between the 1950s and the 1990s but it also provides a working hypothesis for millennial cinema overall. She claims, "We might think of an apocalypse as an ominous prophetic revelation of an intimate, ultimate, cosmic cataclysm that descends in a grandiose and climactic manner […] I would like to define apocalypse simply as this: the end of the world as we know it" (2000, p. 2).

"When man entered the door to the atomic age, he opened the door to a new world. What we'll eventually find in that world, nobody can predict," remarks the doctor-character in *Them!*. It is this precariousness of a new and unpredictable place – "the end of the world as we know it" – that defines the apocalyptic strain of the

Cold War and millennial cycles. In a revised global context – where the countries that had won World War II now had the collective ability to cause massive destruction and even obliteration – a profound shift in consciousness was taking shape. At the same time that many Americans were anxious about nuclear build-up, others were more concerned about the negative effects of Cold War ideologies on ordinary, everyday life. Through policies such as the Monroe Doctrine, the United States was reinforcing an "us versus them" outlook that resulted in internal divisions between "true Americans" and "anti-Americans" (Rogin, 1987, pp. xiii–xvii). Just as 1950s melodrama highlighted the disjunction between the external appearance of material success and an inner emotional anxiety, the apocalyptic films negotiated an ongoing tension between a surface environment and a deeper sense of ideological and spiritual discontentment. As Matthew Frye Jacobson and Gaspar González put it, "the good life and unthinkable death were strangely one and the same" (2005, p. 39).

Both the post-World War II era and the millennium required new ways of thinking and knowing. *Kiss Me Deadly* provides a profitable illustration of this epistemological dimension. The film shows that its protagonist, investigator Mike Hammer, is in way over his head. His usual methods of detecting are failing him, as he cannot see the big picture (the "great whatsit"). By the time he realizes that the world is on the verge of destruction, it is too late. Jacobson and González explain that in *Kiss Me Deadly*, "the unthinkable has already happened" (2005, p. 74).

Though Hammer's story ends rather hopelessly, its overarching theme is that of awakening. The idealistic impulse of apocalyptic cinema often registers as "waking up." In millennial films such as *Magnolia*, characters are surfacing, or re-surfacing, to a new reality that puts into question the ideological values of the 1990s. North America may have been benefiting from increased consumer goods, enhanced research development, and elevated military positioning but many Americans were asking themselves, what was the point of it all? *Magnolia* is motivated by a drive to find "the point" (or at least a point). Its inquiry into the possible existence of a grand design, therefore, insinuates more than a search for meaning. *Magnolia* asserts a desire for a more ethical and open-minded approach to the social issues of its day.

Ideological Awakening in Contemporary Millennial Cinema

The millennial cycle includes apocalyptic cinema as well as related films that convey cosmic, prophetic, or existentialist themes. It encompasses a range of genre offerings, from such dramas or science fiction thrillers as *American Beauty* (1999), *Contact* (1997), *Traffic*, and *Signs* (2002) to the action-spectacles *Armageddon, End of Days* and *The Matrix* series (1999, 2002, 2003), to more provocative fare such as *Dogma* (1999) and *Fight Club* (1999). Many of these titles, particularly the dramas and thrillers, are similar to *Magnolia* in their re-negotiations of conventions of gender and class under the "time pressure" felt at the turn into the twenty-first century. With many, there is also a sense of an inaccessible past, a stable setting of knowledge and identity that is no longer available, if it ever was, even if a promising future may lie ahead. In millennial cinema, according to Sippl, it is the "irretrievability that makes it apocalyptic – the personal and social incapacity to regain what has been lost, even if afforded the ground to begin again" (Sippl, 2000, p. 2).

In most instances, the characters undergo an identity crisis, which represents an examination of current social conditions. They have crossed a point of no return; they believe there is no place for them in society. By way of example, the protagonists in *Signs* and *American Beauty* grapple with a series of questions about the world they inhabit. The answer in *Signs* is the restoration of ideological order. It is the opposite in *American Beauty*, given that the world, as known by the protagonist, must be obliterated. *Magnolia* differs in this respect, refusing to resolve its cultural contradictions and proposing that its characters will continue to negotiate these tensions.

Signs shares *Magnolia*'s existentialist themes yet it provides a contrast in its reassessment of contemporary American social values (Feit, 2004, pp. 134, 139). The protagonist Reverend Graham Hess (Mel Gibson), a disillusioned former Episcopal priest, begins to question his faith after the freakish death of his wife. He leaves his post at the church to work on his farm full time. As mysterious crop circles materialize on his land and the farm animals act increasingly strangely, he and his family begin to believe that extra-terrestrial beings are visiting them and launching an invasion of the planet. In his search for what all of this means, Hess finally realizes that his wife's dying words have given him the tools to battle the aliens. One scene particularly resonates with *Magnolia*'s treatment of coincidence. The priest reasons that some people take unexplainable events as an indication that "there will be someone there for them, and that fills them with hope." For others, these events "could be good, could be bad, but they feel that whatever happens, they're on their own and that fills them with fear."

In this instance, Gibson's character is looking for meaning in an evidently absurd world. He asks, "Do you see signs, see miracles? Is it possible that there are no coincidences?" Like *Magnolia*, *Signs* explores the possibility of a world without chance that is ultimately governed by design. Both examples tap into a broader search for significance and a hunger for faith circulating within millennial popular culture (Feit, 2004, p. 135). However, *Signs* notably reinforces a stable male order. It focuses on a (white, heterosexual) male protagonist who represents authority (albeit an authority in crisis) in his roles as family father and church Father. Given that the wife is deceased, she is relegated to the narrative margins, which centralizes Hess.

In comparison to *Signs*, *American Beauty* offers a more reflexive examination of masculinity while also going further in critiquing structures of capitalism. Feeling alienated and disenfranchised, Lester Burnham (Kevin Spacey) decides to quit his job, rebel against his marriage, and "re-masculinize" his image. He explains, "It's the weirdest thing. I feel like I've been in a coma for about twenty years, and I am just now waking up" (quoted in Tripp, 2005, p. 181). *American Beauty* conveys Lester's journey out of conformity and commodification. He realizes he has become an object within a system dictated by late-industrial capitalism and mass-mediated images. According to Daniel Tripp, this film and many like it, such as *Fight Club* and *The Matrix* are "male epiphany films;" they are "all linked by a common acknowledgement of, and consequential response to, masculinities perceived to be in jeopardy" (2005, p. 181). In *Fight Club*, for instance, the protagonist tries to combat the feminization he perceives – a shift caused by an accelerated capitalist engine – by inspiring other men to participate in a new cult of physically aggressive manhood. In *The Matrix*, the lead realizes that he is not living a real life but rather a simulated one, controlled by computers who are using human body-energy to power their domination of the earth.[4]

In Tripp's view, each protagonist undergoes "an experience of 'awakening' through which he comes to the realization that his life has been automated and/or manipulated by external forces, and that his desire has not been his own" (2005, p. 181). The theme of ideological awakening structures *Magnolia* as well. Yet, this film is less about masculinities in jeopardy than gender identity in flux. As we will see in Chapter 3, femininity and masculinity are represented on a continuum rather than as binary oppositions. These gender constructs are viewed as unstable and fluid, characteristics supported by the principle of "multiplicity" that governs both plot and form.

Nonetheless, even if the film treats gender in more complex ways than in the "male epiphany" narratives, it is beneficial to place *Magnolia* alongside these examples in order to more fully comprehend the roles that class structures and corporatism play. Almost all of *Magnolia*'s male characters are living half-lives, a direct function of the media industry that surrounds them and their own very limited understandings of masculine identity. Given that most of these males work (or have worked) in the television industry (e.g., Earl, Jimmy, Frank, Donnie, Stanley) – and that the technology of television continues to permeate their everyday lives – they are trapped within a world of mechanization and objectification motored by consumer culture. To their own detriment and that of those around them, the male characters are playing out patriarchal models of identity. As Mario DeGiglio-Bellamare puts it, "Their lives represent the pathologies of fame and success in [the television industry]: the career pressures, the competitiveness, the stress, the lying, alcoholism, drug addiction, and, ultimately, the broken confidences of fallen glories and the defeated spirit of shame" (2000). These men are awakened toward a more humanized, humbled position. This occurs with the climactic rain of frogs but also more importantly within the small-scale, deeply felt interactions that build throughout the story.

The adult male conflicts carry devastating consequences for the women and children in the film. Young Stanley, for example, feels the stress caused by his father's expectations. He needs to become a "winner," which will, in some sense, prove his manhood. This desire informs the humiliation he experiences when he pees in his pants while on the television show. Meanwhile, many of the female figures are spinning out of control. *Magnolia* suggests that their chaos is a result of their subordination to men, their lack of self-empowerment, or the (direct or indirect) influence that the media industry has on their personal lives. For some characters, such as Claudia, all three factors shape her struggle. A look at *Magnolia* in the context of other examples in the "male epiphany" category shows evidence of an egalitarian approach to the conflicts of gender, even if the majority of its characters are male. The structure – and logic – of the film pay attention to the way that masculine and feminine norms affect, and are affected by, each other.

Magnolia's depiction of a crisis of faith becomes in part a critique of the consumerist-oriented, media-saturated climate that defines the close of the millennium. To "wake up" is to, in the words of Aimee Mann's accompanying song, "wise up" to the ideological constraints perpetuated by Los Angeles's communications industry. Anderson uses the media backdrop to subtly but implicitly criticize his own business from within. Even more broadly, he concludes that, at the turn into the twenty-first century, various modes of the "self" have been technologized. Like *American Beauty*, *Fight Club*, and *The Matrix*, this musical-melodrama speaks to anxieties about "the extent to which identity is not only always already mediated, but also itself a medium" (Tripp, 2005, p. 182). In *Magnolia*, identity has become a technological "medium," as seen in the inescapable flow of television through public and domestic spaces. Even those who work outside the media cannot escape its effects. Jim Kurring behaves as if he is on camera for an imaginary *COPS*-style program as he sets out on his morning patrol. He may sit alone in his car but he envisions an ever-present, live media stream that requires him to act the role of the rugged individualist. In certain instances, such a state can be both liberating and confining (see Chapter 3).

Magnolia's focus on technology, commerce, identity, and gender signals a relationship that reaches back, beyond its own contemporary millennial moment. Its "fin de siècle" sensibility points to an indebtedness to the late-nineteenth century, a time when modernism and industrialization were gaining momentum. The technological mediation of identity was a central cultural concern then, just as it was a century later. The opening sequence's reference to early cinema (and the Pathé camera) reiterates this interest in the late-1800s and early-1900s. As the film looks toward the future, it calls on the past.

The negotiation of birth, death, and re-birth plays out differently in *Magnolia* than in many "male epiphany" films. Tripp demonstrates that "in both *American Beauty* and *Fight Club*, we are presented with tragic visions where only death, symbolic or otherwise, can allow the male hero to surmount [the problem of] mediation" (2005, p. 184). In *American Beauty*, Lester dies, and has in fact been dead since the start of the story, but his consciousness survives (via his voiceover narration). *Fight Club* ends on a more cynical note, with the implosion of buildings across the Manhattan skyline, an allegorical sign that the capitalist machinery has been (and must be) destroyed altogether if a re-envisioning of masculinity is to be achieved. The unnamed protagonist (Edward Norton) who has struggled against his alter ego for the film's entirety comes to terms with the disintegration of his identity, which has been under attack by corporate values and constant threats against a range of masculine models. According to Tripp, *Fight Club*'s solution is "schizophrenia" while *American Beauty*'s "answer lies in a stable, uncompromised male position" (2005, pp. 185–6). In *The Matrix* series, Tripp says, machine-to-human interface presents the only route out of mechanization, which means that de-humanization is inevitable.

Magnolia, however, sustains a sense of instability and fractured subjectivity while moving its characters into more vulnerable, empathetic, and yet still contradictory positions. In other words, the solution for embattled gender identity does not lie in an eradication of the battle nor does it require a shift toward more coherence or unity. The answer is also not to succumb to a rigid set of social norms. These characters come to terms, simultaneously, with an insecurity intrinsic to any form of identity and their newfound desire to re-invent the ground on which their subjectivity is structured.

To conclude, *Magnolia* understands the cultural anxieties of the millennium as deeply rooted in capitalism and gender relations. It translates broader historical trends of global economic expansion, technological proliferation, and a rise in nationalist violence into concrete, emotional experiences of mass media and male power. The year 1999 presents an opportunity to "wake up;" the film's interstitial weather reports signal "the end of the world as we know it." Yet this may be the best of all potential outcomes. To return to Hipps' proposal that the rain of frogs is perhaps "the only possible conclusion to this story," the surprise flood is not *Magnolia*'s fundamental weakness but rather its greatest strength. Just as the frog rain's inevitability is continually forecast between the visual cracks of the mise-en-scène, the film's call to community emerges from the margins. By the same token, the desire to re-write gender identity is addressed between the lines, in ways that avoid re-inscribing power relations based on stability, unity, and control.

Chapter 2

Through the Viewfinder of a Cinematic "Son"
Reflexivity, Intertextuality, and "Smart Cinema"

While it is problematic to draw clear delineations between mainstream Hollywood cinema and "independent film," *Magnolia* might be best defined as a commercial film with indie sensibilities. A mid-budget, US$35 million picture from New Line Cinema, it has the marks of a "mini-major" production. Such pictures stake a claim to a "personal vision" while explicitly aspiring toward mass distribution and the coveted demographic of 18 to 34 year-old viewers (Kleinhans, 1998, p. 310). Press coverage of Paul Thomas Anderson in the mid-to-late 1990s asserted that New Line had brought the director into its fold in order to strategically emulate Miramax's success with Quentin Tarantino. New Line was the only major studio that had yet to earn an Academy Award nomination for Best Picture; Anderson's image as an artistic neophyte, it hoped, might gain them the respect that would come with an Oscar (Hirschberg, 1999, p. 54). In other words, New Line and Anderson met at the intersection of critically acclaimed, highbrow filmmaking and indie, auteur branding.

In its historical and industrial context, then, *Magnolia* is conversant with many "off-Hollywood" films of the 1990s, including those directed by Tarantino, Wes Anderson, Alexander Payne,

Magnolia, by Christina Lane   © Christina Lane. Published by John Wiley & Sons Ltd

Spike Jonze, Todd Solondz, Richard Linklater, and Kevin Smith. These filmmakers, like Anderson, have "hip" and often "slick" sensibilities. They helped to define a new wave of auteurism, having descended from the 1970s' "film school" generation that included Martin Scorsese, George Lucas, Francis Ford Coppola, Steven Spielberg, and Brian DePalma as well as other 1970s' auteurs such as Woody Allen, Sidney Lumet, and Robert Altman. Many of the recent directors also fit a composite, according to Susan Fraiman, of the cool maverick who represents "an emergent, precarious masculinity produced in large part by youthful rule breaking" (2003, p. xii). This is not to take away from the unconventionality or potential progressiveness of these "bad boys" (2003, p. xii). However, according to Fraiman, many of these rising directors celebrate the cool of "maleness" and rebel against the feminine, which they define as maternal, static, and rigid (2003, p. xvii).

Anderson's relation to this group of filmmakers is complicated and hence so is his association with this trope of coolness. While he is often identified with this 1990s' wave – he was included, for example, in Sharon Waxman's *Rebels on the Backlot: Six Maverick Directors and How They Conquered the Hollywood Studio System* (2005) – he shows a conspicuous interest in the female-identified genre of melodrama, as evidenced in *Magnolia*. In addition, he typically demonstrates a genuine concern for the conflicts faced by the women in his films, depicting them with a complexity that contrasts the work of Tarantino, Wes Anderson, Smith, and others. So while his independence, which is to say his indie sensibility, situates him in the cool camp, his affiliation with female genres and his egalitarian approach to female characters set him apart.[1]

In addition, Anderson shows a general ambivalence toward the father–son narrative that unfolds based on the generational divide between the 1970s' "movie brats" and the 1990s' wave of directors. He resists a predictable staging of the authoritative master and the adolescent "bad boy" by reflexively commenting on the familial relationships he represents on screen. From *Hard Eight* to *There Will Be Blood*, he depicts not so much a struggle by the son to resist the father's legacy as a more far-reaching effort to escape the confines of a traditional father-son narrative altogether. Anderson thus stands out in his relational approach to the forefathers of contemporary American cinema. He knowingly constructs himself as a "son" of 1970s' cinema (and television, for that matter), self-consciously exploring the dual desires to break away from and draw on a "patriarchal" past. As we will see in this chapter, he adopts a range of surrogate fathers, including Altman, Scorsese, Lumet, and Jonathan Demme, through his homages and citations. His also exhibits reflexivity in his casting choices, as exemplified by his decision to put Jason Robards in the role of the dying patriarch Earl (at a time when Robards was succumbing to cancer in real life). Anderson reveals his own ambivalence about the filial position in all of these instances, especially as his career advances. By *Magnolia* (and especially by *There Will Be Blood*), he mobilizes themes of orphanhood and disownment.

Given Anderson's critically minded approach to intergenerational conflicts and patriarchal themes, he is both totally cool and totally uncool. He breaks out of the mold of the adolescent male director who, as described Fraiman, is "indifferent" and "irreverent," most obviously because he cares (2003, p. xi). The director shows deep-hearted concern toward his characters, his films, and his audience. By extension, he posits that the overall medium matters. He refuses to take up the skepticism, cynicism, and nihilism that define so many 1990s' off-Hollywood directors.

A distinguishing characteristic of *Magnolia* is its emotional excess. As a director, Anderson revels in heightened affect. His attraction to emotion becomes crucial when considering the category Jeffrey Sconce labels "smart cinema." In his 2002 essay

"Irony, Nihilism, and the New American 'Smart' Film," Sconce considers a host of 1990s emerging filmmakers. He analyzes such works as *Happiness* (Solondz, 1998), *Your Friends and Neighbors* (Neil LaBute, 1997), *Election* (Payne, 1999), *The Royal Tenenbaums* (Anderson, 2001), *Being John Malkovich* (Jonze, 1999), *Henry Fool* (Hal Hartley, 1998), and *Ghost World* (Terry Zwigoff and Dan Clowes, 2001) as well as Anderson's *Boogie Nights* (1997) and *Magnolia*. Sconce asserts, "Smart cinema is an American school of filmmaking that survives (and sometimes thrives) at the symbolic and material intersection of 'Hollywood,' the 'indie' scene and the vestiges of what cinephiles used to call 'art' films" (2002, p. 351). This cycle has its roots in previous decades of European art cinema and American counter cinema. It also displays the markers of brash, brazen coolness described by Fraiman.

Sconce proposes that this cycle is "marketed in explicit counterdistinction to mainstream Hollywood fare as 'smarter,' 'artier,' and 'more independent'" (2002, p. 350). The distinguishing characteristics are "dispassion, disengagement and disinterest" (2002, p. 359). Acknowledging that these films "do not necessarily subscribe to a uniform textual politics or worldview," he nonetheless claims that, "American smart cinema should be seen as a shared sense of stylistic, narrative, and thematic elements" (2002, p. 358). Such films exhibit a "blankness," which Sconce explains, "can be described as an attempt to convey a film's story ...] with a sense of *dampened affect* (original emphasis)" (2002, p. 359). *Magnolia* could hardly be described as lacking emotion. It is not "blank." Yet it makes a certain claim to "smartness." As this chapter will show, the film qualifies as smart by virtue of its cinematic reflexivity, its attention to themes of fate, its numerous intertextual references, and its deliberate casting. An examination of the reflexivity surrounding Tom Cruise will conclude the chapter. The following contemplation of *Magnolia* as a form of "smart cinema" elaborates and elucidates the productiveness of the smart category.

"This is That Movie": Style, Reflexivity, and Synchronicity

In Sconce's effort to re-define off-Hollywood film style in the wake of the recent wave of new filmmakers, he reconsiders the work of David Bordwell, who has argued that such films often show that they are anti-commercial through cinematic technique. A low budget dictates stylistic choices. For Bordwell, the long take (a common device in art cinema and indie films) results from financial constraints (1985, pp. 206–12). Sconce counters this claim, however, positing that the formal techniques associated with contemporary independent cinema are less about budget than "a deliberate aesthetic" (1985, p. 360). The modernist, art-cinema devices of interruption and distanciation have been replaced by "clinical observation" (1985, p. 360). Such a strategy creates a contrast between indie films and big-budget, studio releases because multiplex movies have moved toward stylistic markers such as acceleration, intensification, and hyper-stylization (1985, p. 360).

Magnolia, however, deploys the techniques associated with expensive Hollywood films more so than the static shots or tableaux set ups associated with a blank "aesthetic." Anderson's sweeping camerawork, traveling shots and fast-paced edits (in the opening vignette, for instance) set him apart from many of his indie contemporaries. His approach, which tends toward acceleration and velocity, only heightens a sense of emotional immersion. He creates a tension between the critical distance (associated with prior generations of counter cinema) and visceral inundation (often

During the seemingly inexplicable rain of frogs, these words insist "but it did happen"

produced by Hollywood blockbusters). His style fits neither the minimalism cited by Bordwell not the clinicism cited by Sconce.

In addition, *Magnolia* solicits spectators who are active and film- and media-literate. Filled with narrative clues and visual information, the mise-en-scène rewards those who pay attention. The film's cues are particularly aimed at those who consider themselves film connoisseurs, not only because of its massive attention to detail but its perceptible intertextuality. *Magnolia* replicates scenes from other films, pays homage to revered directors, honors traditional genres, and draws heavily on both high and low culture. Moreover, using modernist and postmodernist strategies, it addresses audiences who are as well versed in gaming and accessing the Internet as they are in film-viewing.

The countless 8:2 and Exodus-related references, discussed in Chapter 1, encourage spectators to actively survey *Magnolia*'s spatial landscape. The film's roaming camera and multiple visual planes reveal details that provide both information and pleasure for the audience. The constant appearance of anticipatory clues that foretell the rain of frogs serves as but one example of how cinematic style privileges knowledgeable viewers. At the end of the downpour, a tracking shot moves through Claudia's apartment, closing in on a wall, to reveal a small sign that reads, "but it did happen." (This tells us, in case we are not privy, that there have been real-life cases of falling frogs.) If *Magnolia* contains numerous examples of decodable or readable "signs," then this piece of paper serves as a meta-sign, a knowing wink to the audience about the hyper-importance of our own film spectatorship. There are so many visual and narrative cues in the film that Anderson created a now-obsolete website to chronicle all of them. This reinforced the multi-media dimensions of the spectatorial experience. In a some-what circular process, Internet searching became part of the "game" of movie-going.

In addition to the use of formal elements such as mise-en-scène, cinematography, and editing, *Magnolia* engages with "smart cinema" through its inquiry into themes of morality and fate. According to Sconce, smart films exhibit "a fascination with 'syn-chronicity' as a principle of narrative organization" and "a related thematic interest in random fate" (2002, p. 358). *Magnolia* priori-tizes synchronicity by linking together each of its narrative strands. It also relies on fate and fatalism to explore its own ethical dimen-sions, as exemplified by a brief look at the scene in which Linda waits at the pharmacy counter, waiting for several powerful pre-scriptions to be dispensed. Presumably, this is the day that she will facilitate Earl's humane death, at his wish. When the pharmacists continually question her, it becomes clear that they doubt the validity of her prescription request. They grow increasingly patron-izing. Before long, Linda has an outburst that effectively turns the tables on the pharmacists and challenges their authority. She declares, "Mother fucker. You fucking asshole. Who the fuck do you think you are? I come in here. You don't know me. You don't know who I am or what my life is like and you have the balls, the indecency, to ask me a question about my life!"[2]

For Linda, decency is at stake. Her major contention is that these two professionals, who presume to "know better" than she, sit in judgment of her choices. The truth is that Linda may well be about to cross the line and commit a self-destructive act (and in fact she attempts suicide later in the story). However, the point is that these men judge her whether they know the truth or not. If they have done their job by following protocol, why do they continue to question her private life, especially in a patronizing way? In *Magnolia*, the morality (posed here as "decency") of judging matters most. For example, Officer Jim takes a privileged narrative position precisely because he refuses to pass judgment on others. In contrast, when the reporter, Gwenovier, catches Mackey in his web of family lies, Frank's only retaliation is to sit in silence until she asks, "Oh come on, Frank. What are you doing?" "I am quietly judging you," he replies, invoking his weapon of last resort.

In the pharmacy scene, misogyny plays a role in the indecency of the two men (just as it does in the Frank–Gwenovier interaction). Linda's own language crystallizes the sexism implicit in their point of view. It is the pharmacists' moral superiority that pushes her to the brink. If themes of fate and synchronicity are integral to smart cinema, they materialize very concretely in concerns of morality and personal judgment here. In other words, *Magnolia*'s abundance of implicit ethical references takes the form of rather simple interrogatories (such as, what is the right thing to do, right now?; how should we treat those we love, or those we dislike, or those we do not know?; do our small, everyday actions ultimately mean anything?). These ordinary questions, however, often inform and reflect ideological relations of gender, race, and class politics. They link each scene in ways that at first appear to be merely coincidental. Eventually it becomes evident that these are not chance, isolated queries but deliberate intersections.

Magnolia is "smart" in the sense that it rewards alert viewers not with moral superiority but with insight. The audience members' abilities to connect the narrative and thematic dots enable them to see a "fatedness" to the story where others might not. Most of the characters want to be *known* as opposed to judged, and they desire to be accepted as they are by those who know them best. Audiences become part of *Magnolia*'s affective circle – they become "smarter" – by achieving this form of "knowingness" in relation to the characters.

In a further example of reflexivity, the film shows its "smartness" but asserts its affective dimension at the same time. Following Linda's scene, Earl's nurse Phil tries over the phone to convince a "Search and Destroy" sales operator to connect him with Frank. His goal is to help Earl achieve his dying wish, of seeing his son Frank one more time. Phil's connection to the salesman strengthens as the latter reveals that his mother too had cancer (which "synchronizes" them). Phil, in his best effort to mobilize the operator into action, explains:

> I know this sounds silly and I know that I might sound ridiculous, like this is the scene in the movie where the guy is trying to get a hold of the long lost son. You know, but this is that scene. This is that scene and I think they have those scenes in movies for a reason because they're true. You know, because they really happen. And, you gotta believe me this is really happening.

This moment serves as an optimal example of how *Magnolia* is both passionate (rather than "blank") and smart at the same time. It is also significant that the effect of Phil's speech goes beyond cinematic reflexivity; it is more than a straightforward reminder to the audience that we are watching a film. The scene positions us as spectators well versed in movies: most viewers

Phil explains, "This is that scene"

know what it feels to suddenly think to oneself, "this feels just like a movie" or more specifically, "I have just stepped into a cliché."

Anderson explains the origins of this scene in terms of his own ordeal as a son whose father had recently died of cancer; his personal experience with a terminally ill family member motivated the making of *Magnolia*. In an interview with Chuck Stephens, he states, "I was raised on movies. And there come these times in life where you just get to a spot when you feel like movies are betraying you. Where you're right in the middle of true, painful life" (Anderson, 2000, p. 205).

Anderson's comments position him as both a smart-cinema viewer and a smart-cinema director, someone who recognizes the limitations of living in, and buying into, a heavily mediated society. In this way, he actually provokes his audience to question the entire notion of film-smartness. As Jonathan Romney puts it, "Anderson has a special knack of reminding us that we don't know as much as we think we do, especially when we think that we are just watching another movie. He repeatedly overturns our expectations" (2000, p. 46).

"Raised on the Movies": Intertextuality and the Politics of Paternity

One of the most significant factors in *Magnolia*'s film literacy is the process by which Anderson makes numerous references to those directors whom he respects. Affirming intertextual ties to such figures as Robert Altman, Martin Scorsese, Sidney Lumet, and Jonathan Demme, he draws on their cinematic efforts while also formalizing his own sense of inheritance and indebtedness. Viewers may or may not "get" these references to other directors, films, or genres. They may catch some and not others. However, it matters not if the nods are noticed; they help define the *address* of Anderson's work. He envisions knowledgeable and astute viewers as he makes his films.

Anderson's self-construction as a "son" of such surrogate fathers illuminates the complexities of traditional theories of authorship. Though the "cult of the director" often perpetuates the romantic notion that an auteur's film could (and would) have sprung from any era, the homages and citations in Anderson's films signal that an auteur cannot transcend such factors as historical context or industry conditions. Quite the opposite is true: the director is genuinely defined by, and surely bound by, circumstances of time, place, and influence. In fact, it is most intriguing to examine how a director speaks to, for, and about a specific historical moment and, in turn, how the conditions of that moment speak through the director's oeuvre.

Altman represents the most obvious surrogate father-filmmaker for Anderson. The use of multiple storylines, ensemble characters, and a stable repertoire of performers are primary markers of Altman's authorship (as seen in *MASH* (1970) *Nashville* (1975) *The Player* (1992), *Short Cuts* (1993), and *Gosford Park* (2001)). The two directors exhibit an affinity in visual style, particularly through their layering of the visual field (exploiting the background, middle ground, and foreground) and their tendency to create character intersections through elaborate tracking shots (Hudak, 2004). Anderson is inspired by Altman to treat cinematic space according to Andre Bazin's sense of realism (Bruns, 2008, pp. 193–6). He encourages spectators to discover spatial interrelationships on their own by creating noticeable tensions between left-frame/right-frame and between foreground/background. Both Anderson and Altman share a sense of cinematic reality that might feel like cinema vérité but more closely conforms to Bazin's ideal. They construct a window onto a world that sits alongside reality, a tracing that captures "the ambivalence of everyday experience" (Bazin, 1967, p. 38).

In addition to their congruent styles, Altman and Anderson both offer social critiques of highly specialized industries or institutions. Altman, for example, examines country music in *Nashville*, studio film in *The Player*, fashion in *Prêt á Porter* (1994) and dance in *The Company* (2003) (Hudak, 2004). Like Anderson, he also relies heavily on soundtracks and scores to advance his critique of these insular environments. The two directors share similarities in that they tend to create microcosmic communities that speak to broader cultural and ideological conditions.

Anderson has always been vocal about his affiliation with Altman, for instance, telling the *Saturday Telegraph* that his decision to try to re-make Philip Baker Hall into a bonafide star was inspired by Hall's performance in Altman's *Secret Honor* (1984). His self-prescribed role as cinematic son to Altman came full circle when the older filmmaker asked him to serve as stand-by director on his final picture, *Prairie Home Companion* (2008) (Mottram, 2006, p. 448n.37). (The insurance company had requested a back-up for the shoot due to Altman's failing health.) Anderson later dedicated *There Will Be Blood* to Altman.

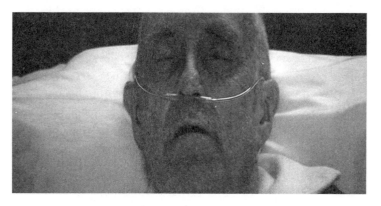

In the final stages of cancer himself, Jason Robards portrays a terminally ill man

The influence of numerous other auteur-figures appears in Anderson's work. Scorsese's centralized attention to patriarchal bonds, male codes of loyalty, and family honor explicitly inform all of the younger director's films. Additionally, Anderson frequently pays homage to Scorsese's cinematography, specifically his striking tracking shots, Steadicam work, and whip pans. (*Boogie Nights*' extended traveling shots take a page out of the 1990 *Goodfellas*, for example.) Demme's *Melvin and Howard* (1980), with its imaginative, performance-driven look at the proverbial American Dream, has relevance for Anderson, as does Demme's penchant for highly subjective camerawork. Demme's repeated patterns of proximity between camera and subject, evidenced for example in *The Silence of the Lambs* (1991), have become a staple of Anderson's visual vocabulary. Additionally, as will be discussed in Chapter 3, Lumet's *Network* provides a template for *Magnolia* on a number of levels.

Anderson pays further tribute to these directors by casting their actors in his films. Jason Robards renders the most obvious instance of such an intertextual citation in *Magnolia*. Not only does he bring to bear a whole host of classical films on his role as Earl, he most significantly played Howard Hughes in *Melvin and Howard*. As noted, Robards' portrayal is also highly reflexive given that the actor was dying of lung cancer while playing the part (of a man dying of lung cancer). He brings an intensity and urgency to his performance, also conveying a kind of symbolic death of the classic body of work – 1960s and 1970s television and film – he represents.

Moreover, a symbolic link exists between Robards and Ernie Anderson. Given the influence on the film of the latter's death, Robards (and Earl) represent significant father images for Paul Thomas Anderson. This dynamic is further reinforced by the fact that the director's father had been in the television industry (as a television personality and announcer). The medium of television often assumes a filial position in relation to the "originating" and "authoritative" medium of cinema; however, *Magnolia* constructs a series of paternal linkages that situate television in a generation of Anderson's predecessors. This suggests two things. First, the director seemingly views himself as a "son" of television (and a purveyor of a subsequent generation of music video, gaming, and Internet media). Second, in *Magnolia*, film and television are not fixed terms; rather they play father and son to each other at various times (giving compelling meaning to the William Wordsworth phrase, "The child is father of the man").

In addition to Robards' portrayal of Earl, a variety of other intertextual casting decisions occur, many of which support a paternal-filial relation between 1960s' and 1970s' filmmakers and performers on the one hand and Anderson on the other. As mentioned, Anderson resuscitated Hall's career in a homage to Altman. Henry Gibson, who appears in *Magnolia* as barfly Thurston Howell (a *Gilligan's Island* reference), starred in four of Altman's productions. Robert Ridgely, who plays the Colonel in *Boogie*

Nights, had acted in two Demme films, including *Melvin and Howard*. In the end credits of *Boogie Nights*, Anderson dedicates the picture to the deceased Ridgely as well as to Ernie Anderson. This "in memoriam" indicates the degree to which the director had emotionally and symbolically linked a whole host of 1960s' and 1970s' actors to his own beloved parent. An array of surrogate fathers thus serve as potential mentors and models.

One particularly reflexive casting choice manifests in Tom Cruise's performance of Frank T.J. Mackey, a self-conscious move that notably sustains father-son tensions in *Magnolia*. As the celebrity spokesperson for a men's movement, Frank, as aptly put by Hannah Hamad, is "a detestable woman-hating hypermasculine egotist misogynist" (2008, p. 37). The role of Frank plays to Cruise's Hollywood star persona, a long line of his screen characters, and his off-screen "real life." (In somewhat similar fashion to Frank, Cruise was abandoned by his father at an early age and eventually ended up at his bedside years later upon discovering that the man was dying.) Mackey – and by extension Cruise – imply a masculine identity that is so overly performative that the performance itself reflects back onto 1980s' and 1990s' Hollywood ideals. The film very specifically extends and comments on Cruise's embodiment of these ideals. The portrait turns on his (on- and off-screen) persona, which is not wounded precisely, but rather indignant, put upon, and often outraged by the actions of ordinary women or men in authority (e.g., *The Firm* (1993), *Jerry McGuire* (1996), *Eyes Wide Shut* (1999)). This *outrage* transforms into *outrageousness* in the depiction of Mackey, which provides a forum for contemplating the star's intersection with gender politics over the course of his career.

In Hamad's analysis of Cruise's trajectory, she observes that he starts as a "pin-up" and "boy-hero" (*Risky Business*, 1983; *All the Right Moves*, 1983), moves into traumatized son roles (*Top Gun*, 1986; *Rain Man*, 1988; *The Firm*, 1993) and, by the mid-to-late 1990s, takes up the image of the post-feminist father (*Jerry McGuire*, *Minority Report*, 2002; *War of the Worlds*, 2005). Hamad explains, "The relationship between fathers and sons has been central to his star image since the mid-1980s, by which time father-son relationships (literal, figurative, or both) had become highly significant to his screen persona" (2008, p. 1). Whether as son or father figure, Cruise distances himself from traditional patriarchal values in ways that illuminate their failings, specifically the "unreliability" and "corruptibility" of male authority (2008, pp. 2, 11). Cruise's masculinity is hence incoherent, seeming to have incorporated second-wave feminist perspectives but with little authenticity or sincerity. According to Hamad, he projects an "immaturity" and "narcissism" that reveal an overall uncertainty about the future of male power (2008, p. 14).

"Immaturity" and "narcissism" define Mackey, who is characterized as dually reactive against feminist politics and the emotionally sensitive "new man" of the 1990s. His enunciation of the Seduce and Destroy program (with guidelines such as "No Pussy Has Nine Lives") ultimately paints him as idealized (by his male followers) yet corrupt and damaged. He offers scripts to his audience, including "how to fake like you are a nice and caring person," teaching them how to act the part of the enlightened (but still hot and sexy) male. Yet with all of his hip-gyrating, pelvic thrusting, and flamboyant kickboxing, his immature and narcissistic qualities are so evidently staged that they enunciate a critique of Frank's persona (within *Magnolia*) and Cruise's persona (outside of it). In this way, "Cruise as Frank" functions as a deconstruction both of the post-feminist "new man" and of Hollywood formulas for heterosexual romance.

For example, from one of his many lesson plans, Frank instructs his audience on how "to form a tragedy" in order to woo a woman into bed. (The "tragedy" that he formulates is the "I just had to put my neighbor's cat to sleep" scenario.) As the crowd of young, rowdy

Frank T.J. Mackey sells his Seduce and Destroy Program

men in the audience hoot and holler with glee, it becomes clear that this tragedy-sketch comes straight out of countless romantic film storylines. The same kind of emotional trial has in fact appeared in numerous Tom Cruise films. The Seduce and Destroy sequences at once highlight the fabricated nature of the "form a tragedy" plan, the manufacturedness of Hollywood boy-meets-girl romance, and the constructedness of Cruise's stardom.

In Mackey's seminar sequences, and throughout, *Magnolia* also plays to the homoerotic undertones associated with Cruise's persona, effecting a broader commentary on 1980s' and 1990s' post-feminism. The television infomercial that introduces Mackey's character underscores his status as a sex symbol (drawing on his 1980s' roles) through camerawork that highlights his pretty face and posing, preening movements. Though he is draped with scantily clad females, the women provide mere window dressing. They are incidental. Frank's focus is on Frank. Post-feminist masculinity relies on male self-obsession as well as eroticized homosociality, both of which structure Cruise's image. The male bonding central to the Seduce and Destroy program only *appears* to hinge on female love/sex objects. Male conquest over women forms a pretense for men's excitement over aggressive masculinity. The infomercial conveys a critical point about both Mackey and Cruise: the central product is Mackey-Cruise. More than his program, Frank sells himself. At this level, the male patrons of Seduce and Destroy desire him (much more so than they desire women). In this context, Mackey-Cruise epitomizes key dynamics of contemporary masculinity in the mass media age.

The interview sequences between Frank and entertainment reporter Gwenovier recapitulate the important relationship between technology and identity. Frank continually attempts to elude questions about his family history in an effort to frame his own narrative. He commercializes himself and his past. Dodging questions about high school, he converts his answers into self-improvement discourse about "leaving the past behind." However, Frank finds himself increasingly disadvantaged by Gwenovier who, within the consumerist terms established by the film, does not buy his story. *Magnolia* grants Gwenovier a degree of narrative authority – she is a knowing character – while Frank underestimates her precisely because she is female and African American. She presents a double threat in the age of post-feminist masculinity, which he misses because he is so taken in by his own performance.

Significantly, the main reason that Frank thinks he "controls the show" is that he is on camera; the television equipment gradually reveals itself through careful frame arrangement. He thinks that this media apparatus enables him to project a self. Yet the television cameras only grant the illusion of control. In reality, *Magnolia* suggests, identity is heavily mediated and technologically inscribed in this millennial age of mass media. Frank believes that these commercial tools work only toward his benefit, not realizing that they contribute to the incoherence and uncertainty of his identity in a post-modern, post-feminist environment.

Magnolia offers a decidedly knowing reading on gender and consumer capitalism through Cruise's embodiment of Mackey. Cruise's stand-out performance is over-the-top, adding to the film's reflexivity. Yet, his enactment is not satirical; it is ironic. The presentation of Mackey-Cruise comes so close to its referent that it can be easily misinterpreted as the genuine article. That is, Mackey-Cruise walks so close to the line of self-obsessive, physically aggressive misogynist that the portrayal can appear to represent a transparent, unproblematized image of both Cruise and post-feminist masculinity. It is so overly performed that one might forget that it is a performance. However, ingrained in *Magnolia*'s portrayal (and embedded in Cruise's performance) there exists a radical internal critique. The film aspires toward a high degree of verisimilitude in its representation of star, character, self-improvement seminar, and infomercial. Call it a "verisimilitude of form," a deep understanding of how underlying codes and conventions of film, media, and masculinity work. In Mackey's storyline, *Magnolia* exercises ironic realism.

The Seduce and Destroy scenes are profitably compared to Jonathan Swift's notorious 1729 essay, "A Modest Proposal." Writing anonymously and responding to Ireland's abject poverty under colonialism, Swift wrote a call to sell children for food as a solution to starvation and overpopulation. Critiquing the government and

the Catholic Church, Swift deployed rhetoric that made the canni-
balization of children seem reasonable, so much so that many read-
ers mistook the essay as an earnest proposition. The essay has been
described "as one of the greatest pieces of sustained irony in the
language" (Ferguson, 1959, p. 473). *Magnolia* mobilizes this con-
ception of irony, insinuating that though it may be a film heavily
immersed in and interested in the mass media, it owes a debt to
literary forms. Therefore, in addition to its status as *media-literate*,
Magnolia affirms a certain *literariness*.

All of these factors – the intertextual use of Cruise, the outra-
geous yet ironic portrayal of Mackey, the reflexive references to
Hollywood gender politics, and the rootedness in literary
rhetoric – contribute to Anderson's self-conscious approach to
the father–son relationship. What appear to be conventional
tropes, such as the father's journey toward redemption or the
son's (subconscious) search for the father, actually operate as pre-
tenses to deconstruct Hollywood oedipal narratives. Even in the
climactic deathbed scene, and even as Mackey ironically forgives
Earl (spewing the epithets "prick," "cocksucker," "fucking asshole"), *Magnolia* closes with a question mark about the logical
conclusion of post-feminist masculinity. As an instance of millennial cinema, the film wonders about the future of father–son relationships, composing a eulogy for the twentieth century,
patriarchal values embodied by a range of fictional characters
(e.g., Earl Partridge, Frank) and real-life figures (e.g., Jason
Robards, Ernie Anderson, Robert Altman).

It is Anderson's dissatisfaction with existing representations
of masculinity – whether embodied by the paternal Robards or
the filial Cruise – that informs *Magnolia*'s themes of disinherit-
ance, disownment, and orphanhood. Many of the characters are
orphans by virtue of the fact that they have disowned their parents. The orphan trope, which will be explored further in
Chapter 5, signals Anderson's interest in escaping traditional or

fixed father–son relationships. *Magnolia* illustrates a desire to deconstruct masculine models even in the absence of alternatives. As we turn to the next chapter, which focuses more exclusively on aesthetics, it will become evident that this impulse toward deconstruction also occurs through an emphasis on multiplicity and fluidity.

Chapter 3

An Aesthetics
of Contradiction
Cinematic Style and Televisuality

A highly stylized film, *Magnolia* relies on distinctive camera, editing, and compositional techniques. Its dominant feature, mobile cinematography, creates an intense relationship between characters, and between characters and camera. The repetition of continuous tracking shots, especially those that move from extreme long shot or medium shot to tightly framed character close ups, works to reinforce themes of community and continuity. The camera traverses time and space, yoking together protagonists and rolling like an emotional wave through each dramatic beat or revelation. Pulled into such close proximity to the characters, we are encouraged to identify with them. Since the cinematography is so consistent throughout – approaching each figure in the same way over and over – a certain egalitarianism predominates in the film, even and especially in its gender representation. This is not a judgmental camera; its moves are sympathetic and relatively impartial.

As a structuring mechanism, the interwoven, fluid cinematic style builds an ongoing relationship between characters and the lens. The cinematography creates a bond not only between the subject and the camera but also between characters and audience, characters and director, and in certain charged moments between

Magnolia, by Christina Lane   © Christina Lane. Published by John Wiley & Sons Ltd

characters and an implied all-knowing power. At times, an omniscient perspective takes over – or at least shares – the overall point of view, though not from an authoritative position. The camera connects with the characters, as they endure their most desperate moments, through movement, angle (often at eye level), and, in particular, closeness.

As this chapter will show, *Magnolia*'s fluid style comes from very specific cinematic techniques, including dolly and crane shots, dissolves, whip pans, and frames-within-a frame. It also adopts modes of rhyming and repetition in its presentation of settings and spaces. There is a sense of mobility and porousness built into *Magnolia*'s editing structure as well. Complex patterns of intercutting create rhythm and pace, leading to two seemingly disparate results: a governing all-knowing presence and a series of free-flowing routes open and available for the spectator. Another source of fluidity is the use of numerous television screens and cameras; the omnipresence of the television medium develops an on-going thread that runs throughout the film.

The conventions of television often dominate, whether in the *What Do Kids Know?* game show or in imagined and simulated television moments. In some ways, *Magnolia* addresses its spectators as a "TV audience" drawing inspiration from the medium's early use of direct address (especially through commercials). This comes across in its "televisual style," an aesthetic approach informed by television codes and conventions. *Magnolia* also incorporates television history, referencing such programs as *COPS*, *The Today Show*, and *Entertainment Tonight* as well as *The Partridge Family* (Earl's last name is Partridge) and *Gilligan's Island* (as mentioned in Chapter 2). The film highlights numerous properties associated with television, such as contradiction, fragmentation, immediacy, seriality, and "dailiness." One of its major structuring devices is "flow," the concept that the television medium presents many bits and fragments while the experience of television (because of its technological flow) often feels continuous and coherent.

The introductory sequence that follows the prologue (the section featuring Aimee Mann's song "One") demonstrates the contradictions of the film's structure and style as well as the centrality of television. The role of Mann's music will be more explicitly addressed in Chapter 4, though this sequence illustrates its importance as well. For now, we turn to an examination of how the "One" sequence launches both an entry point for each main character and an immersion into the formal belief systems articulated by the film. This look at "One" will draw out *Magnolia*'s meta-cinematic qualities. The sequence provides both a contemplation of what cinema can be (implying its relation to a wide range of forms) and an interrogation of simplistic categories within film studies (such as the "classical" paradigm and narrative "closure").

Principles of Fluidity and Flow

In this, the second passage of the film, the prime principles are fluidity and multiplicity. The "One" sequence begins as the preliminary, three-vignette section cuts to black, after a slow track has approached the young boy (the neighbor-witness) of the Sydney Barringer story. In the final lines of the prologue's voiceover, as the camera lingers on a frontal shot of the boy, the narrator summarily remarks, "And for what I would like to say, I can't. This was not just a matter of chance. These things happen all the time." As the framing emphasizes the speechless child (and the chaotic arrest scene that unfolds before him), the words highlight the inchoate status of expression and communication that dominates this point in the film ("And for what I would like to say, I can't"). The theme of the inaccessibility of language, or the incapacity to articulate oneself, is threaded throughout this section and indeed throughout the entire narrative. *Magnolia* represents both an attempt to voice the seemingly inexpressible as well as a proclamation that certain experiences might best be communicated through cinema rather than in any other way.

Following the cut away from the boy, a black screen initiates the opening titles. Simultaneously, the music for "One," first dominated by symphonic keyboard notes, strikes up. As the three main credits ("New Line Cinema presents," "a Ghoulardi Film Company production," "a P.T. Anderson picture") appear over darkness, Mann begins to sing: "One is the loneliest number that you'll ever do. Two can be as bad as one. It's the loneliest number since the number one." The base lyrics – repeated often in the song – frame each character in terms of loneliness and isolation, thereby setting up the story's central conflict.

The tune quickly erupts into percussion and strings as a single image of a magnolia blossoms open and extends its petals (via digital time lapse photography). Next, a superimposition layers the flower over a street map of the San Fernando Valley as well as over the word "Magnolia" spelled out in white, lowercase letters. As the diagram begins to swirl slowly underneath the flower, these merging images appear to generate a sinewy tissue – a proverbial "skin of the film" to invoke a term by Laura Marks – "that looks and *feels* tactile" (original emphasis) (2000, pp. 127–9). This textural surface foregrounds the medium (cinema's possibilities and limitations) while also registering the importance of physical space. (For Marks, "place" functions as a "ground" for identity – it contributes to a sense of embodiment.) This is not to appropriate her term, which is intended to understand better alternative media and marginalized political communities. Rather it is to say that the sequence is dominated by tactility; its skin-like qualities seem to consciously engage notions of place, space, and home, in relation to cinematic specificity.

The television is a focal point in *Magnolia*

Next, a new and barely detectable series of figures emerge from underneath the three superimposed figures: a slow stream of shots from the pending movie appears in near-subliminal fashion. These excerpted still frames include: Phil speaking on the telephone; an audience in attendance at Frank's presentation; two television producers on the game show soundstage; Linda standing in a window frame; and Earl lying on a pillow. These character snapshots, within the symbolic context of the magnolia blossom, effectively convey the metaphor that each relationship matters to one another, like the many petals of a single flower. In other words, the cinematic space is not only grounded in a localized geography but also in a map of social connections and intimate human relationships.

From here, the film cuts to a non-descript living room, indistinguishable from the diegetic domestic spaces inhabited by the characters to come, at the center of which sits a television. The camera quickly pushes in to reveal a program in progress; Frank's infomercial plays to this unoccupied space, selling his "Seduce and Destroy" strategy for winning over women with domination and disrespect. A dissolve moves even closer in proximity to the television image of Frank, leaving behind the living room and entering into the internal world of his show. He continues with his sales pitch until a cut transports us to a tavern, where a broadcast of the program plays in the background on a mounted television set. A medium shot frames Claudia as she sits at the bar in a solitary stupor. The camera tracks forward – rhyming its movement from the previous two scenes (living room and infomercial) – into Claudia's close up at the very moment that a strange man approaches her with an obvious proposition. The next edit takes us to her apartment, with a series of repeated dollies forward that convey she has brought the stranger home. Frank's program plays on as Claudia snorts cocaine in her dimly lit living room and it is revealed that the man sits waiting for the signal that she will now give in to his sexual advances. Cut to: the two of them having intercourse on a bed as the camera tracks in and up toward a picture frame on the wall.

In the reflection of the glass, yet another television segment unfolds. This time, however, it is a promotion for the *What Do Kids Know?* show and, specifically, Jimmy Gator's long career in the industry. Photos of Jimmy cascade on the dual surface – the reflected image of the presumed television screen onto the hanging picture – as he is hailed "an American legend." The film will soon disclose that not only is Jimmy Claudia's father but that they have a tumultuous relationship. Later revelations suggest that many of her insecurities stem from sexual abuse she suffered at his hands as a child. That these images of Jimmy appear on the wall above her bed, and that their source is unclear (do they emanate from a television set or from Claudia's own mind?), gives Jimmy's photo stream an ambiguous and fragmented status. It hovers over her like a floating specter, implicating her father as the cause of her psycho-sexual and emotional concerns. In this instance, the free-flowing camera coincides with the permeability of the mise-en-scène (the merging screens) to reinforce Claudia's own loose, fractured point of view.

Significant here is the concept of television "flow," originated by Raymond Williams and elaborated by John Fiske. They suggest that the experience of television viewing simulates the technology itself, taking the shape of a continuous but often incoherent series of fragments (Fiske, 1988, p. 105; Williams, 1974, pp. 86–96). According to Fiske, "the movement of the television text is discontinuous, interrupted, and segmented" (1988, p. 105). "Fractured forces" govern television, on a textual level, yet it can often feel continuous and free-flowing. This means that "through flow, discontinuity on TV is turned into its opposite: continuity" (Dienst, 1994, p. 30). In *Magnolia*, the continuous television broadcast, coupled with the on-going song by Mann, create this sense of flow. The airwaves and sound waves give continuity to these seemingly separate narrative and spatial fragments.

The notion of flow takes on even more nuanced contours with the next transition as the Jimmy Gator promotional segment continues but the camera moves into the game show host's office. The lens tracks forward toward Gator as he engages in casual sex with a showgirl. The television voiceover proclaims that "he is a family man who has been married for over forty years" while we watch him – within *Magnolia*'s filmic space rather than the television's – engage in apparently illicit and tawdry sex. As we hear that "he is the proud father of two children and one bouncing baby grandchild," a dolly shot takes us forward into a close up of his family

This family photo provides an inaccurate reflection of Jimmy's family

portrait. Articulating the tension between the narration and the visuals – between Jimmy's external image and his real-life actions – this shot sequence highlights hypocrisy but also contradiction. It therefore brings out two more characteristics associated with "flow." As a way of questioning Jimmy's status as a "proud father," the camera movement ends by tightening its field on father and daughter standing side by side in this seemingly idyllic photograph. The framing momentarily constructs a dualistic tension between the characters' familial bond *and* their interpersonal conflict by isolating them within this frenetic play of images.

In a way that extends the television symbolism even further, we suddenly find ourselves back in the original living room (after a brief scene that shows Gator, accompanied by his wife, checking in for a doctor's appointment). Repeating its forward track toward the television set, the camera reveals yet another broadcast. The *What Do Kids Know?* program plays as Stanley, in the role of contestant, proves to be unstoppable. Rapid dissolves move us through his series of correct answers, quickening the pace and mimicking the heated pressure the child obviously feels as the top winner. A sound cue, the ringing of the game show's bell, transports us to Stanley's home as he rushes to get out of the door. He is framed by an unsteady, handheld camera, which reiterates the relentless, frenzied tension of his daily life. As he and his father make their way to school, it becomes clear that the boy is both prized and reviled by his Dad, who aspires (to little avail) to be in the entertainment industry and disapproves of Stanley's bookishness.

As the sequence continues, and "One" plays on, the living room takes center stage again. Though the basic backdrop appears to be the same, with walls and window in the same formation as before, the furniture, television, and wall decorations indicate a shift in time. Now located in the late-1960s, this set up provides a portal into a *What Do Kids Know?* program from the distant past. A very young Donnie Smith gives winning answers and receives the monetary prize. Words on the screen register that it is 1968. With the next cut, we see an adult Donnie "today" preparing to be fitted for braces. Several shots later, we watch him drive distractedly into the glass doors of a convenience store. This introduction to his character uses shorthand to show that he has yet to grow up; he is in fact less mature than Stanley.

The character introductions continue as the camera moves into Earl's home. Phil, arriving for his morning nursing shift, is introduced through a quick whip pan as he surges toward Phil's bedside and then affectionately asks, "How's today then?" An embittered Earl curses. As he inhales, the camera appears to enter his mouth, as a dissolve transfers to an image of his lungs – a brief special effects sequence that figures his cancer as both cartoon and industrial film. (His lungs first appear as an animated series of bronchial tubes and lobes, and then on a medical slide as part of an instructional presentation.)

The slight interruption effected by this animation serves to foreground yet again the film form in terms of its limitations and possibilities. Consistent with its fluid structure, *Magnolia*'s cinematic approach incorporates animation, slide photography, and industrial footage, highlighting its representational repertoire. Given that the

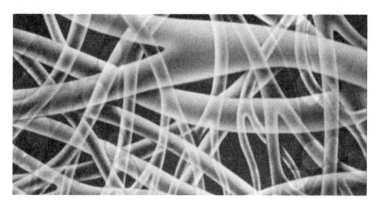

A picture of Earl's lungs

origins of the film term "animation" hark back to the root word "anima," connoting breath, life, and the soul, this brief digression underscores *Magnolia*'s broader preoccupation with life, death, and immortality – its overall millennial crisis. Cinema, in this equation, depicts living, breathing, and also changing. *Magnolia* is not merely interested in film's origins – the birth of cinema – but also in its ever-fluctuating nature, which encompasses still photography, animation, video, electronic broadcast, digitality, and more.

The theater, which is also a tradition closely linked to film, plays a central role in the subsequent scene that focuses on Linda. As she paces through the Partridge home and speaks on the telephone, the camera accentuates her theatrical qualities. It follows her activity by traveling unencumbered through the space occupied by Linda and Earl, portraying their domestic sphere as a performance stage. The house looks more like an artificial set with movable walls and glamour lighting than a family home. This context magnifies Linda's status as a melodramatic (and sometimes histrionic) character while adding a certain critical distance to Earl's deathbed scenes. Earl and Linda genuinely experience their roles as dying patient and nerve-wracked caregiver yet they are also playing their parts to the hilt, somehow caught up in and unable to escape the very media-machine upon which they have built their material lives.

As the "One" sequence finally ends, it returns to television as a reference point. Officer Jim drinks his morning cup of coffee while sitting in front of a broadcast of the *Today* show, a gesture that situates him as the epitome of mainstream, middle-class America. A satisfied viewer, he chuckles at the easy banter between morning show hosts Matt Lauer and Katie Couric, before moving through his daybreak routine. As Mann's song continues to play off-screen, we hear Jim's self-description in an outgoing voicemail message for a dating service. He presents himself as quite simply a good guy, with few pretensions and little emotional baggage. Jim Kurring appears to be the counterpart of Jimmy Gator, as the former strives to avoid hypocrisy and aims to do good deeds. The fact that they share the same first name only highlights their opposition, while further articulating Claudia's ultimate dilemma upon meeting the Officer. Can she trust "Jim" having been exploited so by "Jimmy"?

The "One" sequence closes as Jim receives his morning instructions with his fellow officers at the station, in an image of daily roll call that resembles the ritualistic "let's be careful out there" scene of the classic television series *Hill Street Blues*. In one final television reference, he sets out in his police cruiser and dialogues to himself, as if participating in a television interview, about what it means to be a good cop. As Cynthia Fuchs has noted, "It's like he's in an episode of *COPS*. It speaks to the pervasiveness of the series – as a concept and a cultural condition – that even if you haven't seen *COPS*, you likely have a sense that it informs Jim's self-understanding" (2000). Jim's "act" for the imagined camera serves several functions. As further character exposition, it underscores his role as moral anchor. Unlike the standard *COPS* interior car scene, which offers little insight into the police-characters' genuine thoughts but rather a window into their various modes of self-presentation, this micro-moment provides access to Kurring's true character. He will become an emblematic role model – cherished by the narrative – for his desire "to correct a wrong, or right a situation." (However, as the film will show, he makes mistakes too, as when he dismisses the rap by Dixon.) In this process, then, the scene both incorporates the cinema-vérité codes of reality television while simultaneously commenting on and critiquing the show's heavily mediated format. *Magnolia* mines the artifice of the series in an effort to re-locate and perhaps re-discover a genuine truth – an underlying reality about Jim's (moral) character.

Televisual Strategies

As illustrated by the "One" sequence, *Magnolia* treats television as both content and form. In addition to the technology's appearance as recurring prop (television monitor) and setting (the game show, the infomercial), the television medium is embroidered into the film through formal elements such as camerawork, cutting, and sound. This sequence elucidates the tension between cinema and television, a mediation in its own right as well as a mark of ambivalence toward two technologies that have both competed and collaborated since television's inception. In other words, television is both a solution and a problem for film, thereby playing a central role in *Magnolia*'s preoccupation with the limits and possibilities of cinema. (Television may present both a solution and a problem for the director as well, given that Anderson has family roots in the industry and trained as a production assistant in television.) There is a repeated blurring of television boundaries, as when we see a screen-within-a screen or when one image collides with another. In such examples, a "hall of mirrors" effect occurs suggesting that television can both free up and confine film.

It is well worth examining the ways that television informs both the style and structure of *Magnolia*. It has been observed that the film exhibits a "televisual style" as well as the narrative structure of soap opera (Fischer, 2008; Dillman, 2005; Fuchs, nd). *Magnolia's* televisuals, seen for example in the *COPS*-style soliloquy or the *Entertainment Tonight*-style segment on Jimmy Gator, register at times as continuity (in what feels like streaming or channel-surfing) and at other times as discontinuity (jump cuts or disorientation). In terms of style, Fuchs explains that, as it "swoop[s] in and out of characters and events and settings and times, the film resembles three hours of channel surfing, but this familiar activity becomes loaded with passions, ruminations, and romances. It's TV on a bizarre kind of moral-emotional hyperdrive" (nd). The accelerated cinematography and intense editing increase the intimacy already associated with the medium, capitalizing on the melodrama by making it visceral and immediate. Furthermore, the constant camera movement, as much as it seems "cinematic" in its fluidity, also emulates the spatial and temporal mobility of television viewing.

In addition to its televisual style, *Magnolia* structurally mimics the multiplicity and seriality of television. Joanne Clarke Dillman suggests that the film is grounded in a variety of television strategies such as "dailiness" (2005, p. 146). Television is "daily" in the sense that it plays an integral role in our ordinary, everyday lives. We have come to experience it just as any other part of our lived experience, as realistically as we perceive a neighbor, a custom, or a habit. As Roger Silverstone suggests, "Television accompanies us as we wake up, as we breakfast, as we have our tea, and as we drink in bars. It comforts us when we are alone. It helps us sleep" (1994, p. 3). The character introductions in the "One" sequence resonate here, as though television helps trace a pathway through such morning, noon, and night routines. In its "emulation of real time," *Magnolia feels* like everyday life (Dillman, 2005, p. 146). The soap opera's "infinitely expanding middle" – its constantly evolving and elaborating second act – also informs the film, contends Dillman (2005, p. 146).[1] *Magnolia* starts "in medias res" and spends the bulk of its screen time in the midst of rising action, with many conflicts left unresolved at the end.

Magnolia's emphasis on multiplicity also effects characterization by de-centering the many protagonists. Subjectivity is dispersed. Bruns makes the case that, rather than "giving us a theater of cruelty," staged around power or pain, the film presents a "theater of vulnerability" (2008, p. 203). In this space, the "characters are called out of the safety and comfort of their own little worlds in order to experience" their own "minorness" (2008, p. 203). He refers to the work of Stephen Benson, claiming that they "[face] up to [...] the constitutive otherness and heterogeneity of subjectivity" (Benson, 2003, p. 295, quoted in Bruns, 2008, p. 203).

The film's fluidity, and specifically its open-endedness, play a critical role throughout. Temporally, it both collapses and extends the narrative, continually suspending the story in mid-moment. Dillman remarks that "from cut to cut and from segment to segment, time in the interlocking narratives stands still" (2005, p. 146). She cites one notable example from the first hour in which a cut takes us away from the action at Claudia's door (where Kurring knocks in an effort to gain entrance) just after she has said, "Just a second, I have to get dressed." From there, the sequence follows Linda, then Phil and Earl, then Frank, Donnie, the game show, Gator, and then back to Claudia's apartment, culminating in her opening the door and granting access to the policeman. "Time seems to happen continuously rather than sequentially," according to Dillman (2005, p. 146).

In another instance, Phil remains on a seemingly never-ending telephone call with Frank Mackey's staff as numerous scenes unfold with other characters. The extended phone conversation, characterized by "holds" and silences, heightens the suspense over Phil's

An open-ended final shot of Claudia

quiet and purposeful mission while also taking the shape of an actual lifeline (to invoke quiz show *So You Want to be a Millionaire*) in which Earl Partridge's emotional and physical life hangs in the balance.

Magnolia's seriality is also evident in its approach to character resolution. Some of the protagonists experience closure (or mini-closure) while some do not. Earl dies; Gator loses his life in a fire; Phil re-unites Frank with Earl; Donnie experiences an epiphany; Claudia and her mother embrace; and Stanley takes a minor though important stand against his father. On the other hand, the murder in Marcie's apartment goes unresolved and Frank's familial relationship with Linda remains tenuous (albeit improved). The final moment between Claudia and Jim, the characters who (according to most observers) constitute the heart of the film, recapitulates this predominant tension between resolution and seriality. A behind-the-shoulder shot frames Jim as he sits on her bed and they have a placid conversation that is inaudible to the viewer. With Claudia in mid-sentence, a cut to black ends the scene, leaving them in the midst of their lives – and their relationship. As Olsen describes, "Waiting for something, anything to lift them up, two unlikely souls come together in one moment of genuine connection: Claudia Gator, seen quite literally in a different light, smiles brightly at the arrival of Jim Kurring, and the fog of her trouble burns off, if only for an instant" (2000, p. 28).

Dillman explains that "the last shot of the film, the close-up on Claudia's face, seems to end abruptly despite all the time the film has already consumed" (2005, p. 147). The final cut to black may be unexpected but it sustains the point repeatedly made in *Magnolia* that conflict is continuous and contiguous. It is more about people than plot. That is, these stories are relationship-oriented and relational. The fact that Claudia and Jim's conversation is too low to be fully discerned reinforces this notion. While the conversation of the film is about to conclude, that of this couple has only begun. It extends the conversation of all of their previous relationships and conflicts.

Tension and Contradiction

Although scholars have appropriately problematized a number of originary ideas from film and media studies, many of these foundational formulations often persist, explicitly or implicitly. For example, a "lack of closure" is often associated with counter cinema or television, even when it characterizes numerous films. Seriality still connotes television, even when it also structures much classical and contemporary cinema. Television is often assigned a "feminine" role even when we know that gender implications are more nuanced than this. *Magnolia*'s approach to such concepts as closure, seriality, television, and even classical Hollywood film, implies that it acknowledges these concepts' complexities even when their academic use often appears to reduce or simplify them. In other words, *Magnolia* shows the way toward complicating many formulations that preoccupy the field of film and media studies. It is all too easy to lapse into an oppositional thinking that pairs up: Hollywood with the classical paradigm; seriality with television; film with masculinity; and television with femininity. *Magnolia*, with its emphasis on multiplicity, fluidity, and contradiction, questions such corollaries and acknowledges its own origins, especially within previous Hollywood films that have multiple storylines, serial structure, or more than one protagonist.

Magnolia, therefore, encourages us to question the ground on which much early scholarship was built, especially concerning the paradigm of "classical Hollywood cinema." For example, scholars David Bordwell and Peter Wollen posit respectively that most Hollywood films adhere to practices of cause and effect, linearity, and closure. For Bordwell, "Hollywood story construction" is based on "causality, consequence, psychological motivations, the drive toward overcoming obstacles and achieving goals" (Bordwell, Staiger, and Thompson, 1988, p. 13). Wollen defines mainstream film in terms of "narrative transitivity, single diegesis and protagonist, closure, pleasure, transparency, hierarchy of discourses, and identification" (Wollen, 1986, p. 120, quoted in Dillman, 2005, p. 142). Yet these characteristics often constitute the exception rather than the norm.

The classical examples that are most often used to substantiate paradigms of narrative structure, such as *Gone with the Wind* (1939), *His Girl Friday* (1941), *Casablanca* (1942), or *Rear Window* (1954), can just as easily be read alternatively. They resist cause and effect logic, linearity, transparency, and/or closure. In each of these instances, a basis exists to argue against causal logic and closure. By the same token, each of these films might be described as having more than one protagonist or more than one subjective point of view. *Magnolia*'s style and structure honors the complexity of classical cinema. Not only does this film defy categories such as the "classical Hollywood paradigm," it also reflexively highlights the heterogeneity of the classical era. While not perhaps immediately apparent, its implicit illumination of overly rigid accounts of Hollywood structure relates to the previously discussed themes of birth, death, and re-birth. Anderson offers a contemplation of "cinema in crisis" – an inquiry into the medium at the millennium – in a way that acknowledges that *Magnolia* too is steeped in prior Hollywood traditions of multiplicity, tension, and contradiction.

Magnolia also pays homage to the conversation between film and television by citing a source from post-classical Hollywood. In an example of the intertextuality explored in Chapter 2, the film makes references to Sidney Lumet's treatment of television in the 1976 *Network*. This Academy Award nominee for Best Picture marked a turning point in Hollywood's understanding of television as a multi-national, mass media phenomenon. A satirical yet serious drama devoted to a full-fledged critique of the corrupt monopolization of the medium, *Network* employs a television aesthetic – a televisual structure and style. *Magnolia* extends respect to this picture through its mobile camerawork, narrative voiceover, and most specifically its visual look. The game show, in particular, draws from *Network*'s nightly live broadcast of Howard Beale (Peter Finch). It also refers to the former film through its repeated attention to screens and monitors. This is particularly noticeable in *Network*'s beginning, which opens with a display of numerous network broadcasts and then tracks forward to the Union Broadcasting System channel, an action the camera reverses at the end.

In its invocation of *Network*, *Magnolia* internalizes and endorses the underlying ideological critique of capitalism. As a descendant, it does not so much re-work or renovate as it reiterates the earlier film's concerns about the pervasive, inescapable, and alienating power of the industry. The problems with television – its conglomerate structure, its cynicism, its move toward infotainment – have only accelerated and intensified, suggesting that *Magnolia*'s characters are the begotten children of *Network*'s ensemble.[2] This context deepens our understanding of *Magnolia*'s overall cinematic style and televisuality. Through multiplicity, fluidity, and contradiction, Anderson critiques media industries from within, deploying familiar codes of film and television as he considers media's role in society.

Chapter 4

Sound and Voice
De-Centering Meaning

Just as *Magnolia* shows the influence of multiple technologies, the film incorporates a range of genres. Prior discussions have examined its relation to melodrama and the disaster movie, yet it is also heavily shaped by the musical. *Magnolia* is a musical in so far as it uses sound to express conflict, reveal character, and forge connections between scenes. The music is central to the story's excess, given the ways in which the instrumental score (by Jon Brion) and a host of individual songs generate intense affect. Specifically, this chapter will consider how the folk-pop music of Aimee Mann contributes to *Magnolia*'s emotional setting. The segments that include Mann serve as intermittent centerpieces, usually playing out during the most heavily edited and quickly moving sequences. Her lyrics and her voice provide a critical link between characters and scenes. Like signposts that appear to help us make sense of an apparently rugged terrain, they bring into relief and interpret the overall topographical map of the film.

Mann's eight songs (plus "Deathly") are all original except for her cover of Harry Nilsson's "One."[1] According to Anderson, "having one voice to unify it all seemed like a good idea" (Olsen, 2000, p. 26). In actuality, though, Mann's music poses a challenge to the concept of unity. It contains many inherent tensions, which open up the logic of the film, and disperse multiple meanings across the narrative field. In keeping with *Magnolia*'s reliance on fluidity, multiplicity, and contradiction, the songs complicate the narration, presenting questions about the authority or singularity of authorial "voice" as it is ordinarily conceived.

Magnolia's music offers insight into the film's overall de-centeredness. As this chapter will show, the film itself is "polyphonic" (according to John Bruns), containing many independent but equally important narrative strands. The multiple points of view help to create an ethical dimension in which the moral and social order is questioned. Viewers are encouraged to come in close proximity to the characters. They are asked to be vulnerable with them and with themselves. The film posits a world of social responsibility in which each character examines his or her own accountability. As a result, even seemingly peripheral figures take on crucial significance. Mann's own vulnerability – and the message of survival and struggle she conveys in her voice and lyrics – help to construct *Magnolia*'s ethical space.

An oft-told anecdote is that Anderson, who had known Mann for several years, began writing the *Magnolia* screenplay while listening to a demo recording of her unreleased (and then still-in-progress) songs. Hence, the creative process that spawned both the film and Mann's album was organic and reciprocal. Mann explains, "[Anderson] heard the record I was working on and was really excited about some of the songs and started working on a screenplay. Then I would read some of the screenplay and play some music and fit it in thematically. There were a couple of songs that were written that way, back and forth" (Bessman, 1999, p. 46). For example, the director used the opening line of the musician's song "Deathly" (which does not actually appear in the film) as a dialogue beat in the first date between Claudia and Jim (Claudia remarks, "Now that I've met you, would you object to never seeing me again?") This sentence in fact provided an initial kernel that inspired Anderson to write the script. (He explains, "I heard that line and wrote backwards" (Anderson, 2000, p. viii). While the beat, as spoken, sounds a bit clunky on screen, it serves as a thesis statement for the film – a reiteration of the vulnerabilities at stake for each character – and therefore perhaps should not be judged "as dialogue" per se.

As noted by many reviewers, Anderson "adapts [Mann's] music […] for the screen much like adapting a book" (Hunter, 2000, p. 115). In fact, the songs function in various ways – as source text, filmic environment, and authorial voice – while also forging a separate "character" within the film. According to Dillman, the singer's role as "another character" translates into "a counter-narrative strategy" (2005, p. 144). She states, "the predominance of a strong female voice working against and at times doubling the text […] points to *Magnolia*'s challenge to the male textual system and more traditionally 'masculine' narratives" (2005, p. 144). We need not necessarily subscribe to the notion that Hollywood cinema is an inherently "male system," to profit from Dillman's astute proposition. To re-frame Dillman slightly, Mann does in fact represent a woman's voice, to the extent that her songs and experiences come from her. Yet, she also helps to mediate various characters' experiences. In this way, Mann's subjective voice assumes a role every bit as important as the camera, mise-en-scène, or editing, as an interpretive lens that conveys affect and character revelation. "One" offers a considerable example of how Mann speaks to and for the characters, articulating their central conflicts, which revolve around loneliness and disconnection.

Mann's presence grounds the film emotionally while also situating it as Los Angeles-based. According to James Hunter of the *Village Voice*, in one song, "Build That Wall," "[She pulls] a transcendently vocal manner out of undifferentiated layers of

L.A. living room goth" (2000, p. 46). He goes on to say, "She seems to own the nerve endings of the city behind her songs" (2000, p. 46). Hunter captures both the deep, visceral impact of Mann's breathy style and emphasizes the way she helps to paint the setting – to stage the scene – with her lyrics and voice. These compositions thereby translate a geographical space into an emotional one. In addition, they contribute to *Magnolia*'s serial structure while simultaneously fostering a pattern of continual expansion and contraction. As Hunter puts it, "Mann sings about frequent emotional closings-down in a melody that opens up with all the aesthetic symmetry of the Southern flower of Anderson's title" (2000, p. 46).

Positioning Mann

This consideration of Mann's "voice" as both narrative and narrational device gives way to a nuanced understanding of authorship. Within a film that registers a number of significant voices (e.g., actors' performances, the opening VO by Ricky Jay, the orchestral score by Jon Brion), Mann and Anderson generate two central authorial threads. Their process during the early phases of conceptualization underscores the collaborative foundations of *Magnolia*. At times, they seem to rhyme or echo while, at others, they radiate or diverge. This creates a layered texture, implying that Mann serves less a unifying function than one that challenges the notion of a unified or singular logic. Bruns proposes, "Overtly self -conscious and unapologetically artificial, [Mann's "Wise Up" song] functions to undermine the possibility of a simultaneity with unity" (2008, p. 208). She de-centers the film both narratively and ideologically, contributing to the gender fluidity noted in previous chapters.

The music video for "Save Me," directed by Anderson as a compendium to the film, magnifies Mann's multiple positions and stresses her authorial role. In this video, Mann appears alongside various individual characters within the film's diegesis. More specifically, characters take up positions within the very mise-en-scène that they occupy in *Magnolia*, but none of these shots appears in the film. These are slightly altered stagings of existing scenes, composed to include the singer and allow her to sing to and for the protagonists. (The characters do not sing.) She thus functions as both chorus (vocalizing their interior preoccupations) and witness (validating their experiences). She is both spokesperson and attendant, corroborating and testifying to their emotional conflicts. As a result of being the thread that joins each shot, Mann comes to represent the affective logic of this video while aiding in its "flow" into the wider film.

As Mann's songs are informed thematically by emotional dysfunction and addiction, it is possible to identify them reductively with "self-help" discourse (and with the psychology-based and self-focused connotations that are often implicated therein). However, upon close listening, it is clear that even within her songs an internal dialogue takes place – she is both confused sufferer and knowing wise-woman. Put another way, she exhibits a dual over involvement and critical distance in ways that recall (and perhaps inspire) Anderson's filmmaking style. According to Thomas Bartlett, "she manages to be victim and savior at the same time, and the trick, I think, is in her voice, warm with intimacy but always somewhat detached from the stories she tells, touched with a chill of cynicism, unimpressed with her own emotional vulnerability" (2005). Mann, therefore, activates tensions between interior and exterior. She interrogates the weaknesses and strengths in individuals in ways that can refer out to ideological and institutionalized power. She too participates in a "theater of vulnerability" that pulls one out of her "own little world" into a more socially engaged and communal experience. She presents a corollary to the smart film by producing the "smart song."

Mann also embodies "a victim and a savior at the same time" in her professional career. Having had success in the 1980s as lead singer for the new wave band 'Til Tuesday (achieving a hit with "Voices Carry"), she faced considerable corporate resistance throughout the 1990s as she struggled to become more independent and she has gained a reputation as a defender of artists' rights against the controlling interests of the music industry. The positive response to the *Magnolia* soundtrack – and the Grammy and Academy Award nominations she won with it – fed into a comeback narrative through which Mann is finally redeemed for both her suffering and resistance (paralleling the film's themes of redemption). In this context, her status as "troubled" and "wounded" (prior to the picture's success) reverberates within and through the characters. Her public fight against corporate music and the launch of a self-produced label (SuperEgo Records) in the same year as *Magnolia*'s release resonate with its message of resistance, struggle, and transformation.

One of the film's most significant musical sequences takes place just after Earl's speech about regret (which will be analyzed in the next chapter). Here, the camera connects numerous protagonists as they individually sing Mann's "Wise Up." The initial piano chords commence as the camera focuses on Phil, who has just mercifully administered a lethal dose of morphine to Earl. A cut to Claudia accompanies the first lyrics, as she half-sings along with Mann. At first, it is not obvious whether the song plays diegetically or non-diegetically. Is Claudia vocalizing to a track that plays in her apartment or is the music external to the scene? By its end, the sequence will have featured nine characters, moving from Claudia to Jim to Gator to Donnie to Phil/Earl to Linda to Frank to Stanley. According to Anderson, the goal was for the musical sequence to simulate a natural radio-listening experience. He declares, "Haven't you ever sung along to a song on the radio? In the simplest way, it's just that" (Olsen, 2000, p. 27). The sequence is thus meant to reinforce verisimilitude but also to communicate the "dailiness" previously described.

The "Wise Up" sequence offers a further example of the porousness of this film text. The protagonists and settings lose their boundaries as the "song baton" is continuously passed from one character to another. The slow fade-in makes it difficult to tell that the sequence is indeed starting. Anderson states, "I thought the best way to do that sequence was to have it creep up on you [...] By the time it cuts to [Jimmy Gator], you've been hoodwinked into a musical number!" (Willman, 2000, p. 67). This causes an uncomfortable interruption that is at once less sudden and more abrupt than an obvious break in an ordinary musical. The conspicuous moment has been criticized by some, such as Janet Maslin who calls it "the great uh-oh moment" of an otherwise exceptional film (1999, p. E15). It has been touted by others such as Pauline Reay who celebrates its expressivity. Reay suggests that "Wise Up" works on two levels by articulating each character's point of view while furnishing commentary about them (2008, p. 65). Successful or not, the sequence follows in the form of the rest of the film; it is not a breakaway moment.

As the piece builds, growing louder and faster, an internal dialogue develops. The chorus ("It's not going to stop/It's not going to stop/'Til you wise up.") emphasizes a noticeable tension between empowerment and powerlessness. This is accentuated as it concludes, with Stanley sitting alone in a darkened library, singing:

> It's not going to stop
> No, it's not going to stop
> 'Til you wise up.
> No, it's not going to stop
> So just give up.

The question of "wising up" versus "giving up" reiterates the self-knowing and critically engaged attitude of Mann's music discussed before. Her songs are wise enough to know that there is strength in vulnerability.

In her analysis of *Magnolia*'s use of music, Reay demonstrates that each set of lyrics is tied to the featured character's emotional struggle. "For example," she writes, "Jimmy sings the lines about finding a cure which can be related to his illness and also to his problem relationship with Claudia. Donnie sings the line about drinking linked to the key scenes in the bar when his inner feelings are revealed [...]" (2008, p. 65). The closely matched compositions and the sequence's overall connective approach distinguishes it as the most obvious place where "*Magnolia*'s vast array of disparate plots and unrelated characters" are brought together (Borrelli, 2000). This confirms the film's process of prioritizing thematic linkages over story- or character-driven associations. Yet, even this – the most obvious instance of unity – communicates a central tension between coherence and fragmentation.

Magnolia as Polyphonic Film

This multiplicity seen in Mann's "voice" and the "Wise Up" sequence relates to Bruns' proposition that *Magnolia* is a "polyphonic film." Drawing on an understanding of sixteenth century "plainsong" (also known as the Gregorian chant), he contends that this "principal form of musical composition" informs not only the audio design of Anderson's work but also its narrative and thematic structure. In defining polyphonic music, he borrows terminology from Arthur Tillman Merritt for whom the form "is made up of independent lines, not absolutely free of each other but good individually, and at the same time accommodating themselves to an ensemble over which no one of them is unduly dictatorial" (Merritt, 1939, p. 3, quoted in Bruns, 2008, p. 190). The multi-vocal perspective in *Magnolia* – and its egalitarian approach to characterization (where even minor figures can take on major significance) – makes it a prime example of polyphony. Its lack of center leads to a re-consideration of the film's power relations.

A musical analogy works well to explain the film's visual and narrative technique because, as Bruns posits, "Like music, the cinema is to be grasped by feeling its rhythms rather than by understanding its signs" (2008, p. 194). *Magnolia*'s mobile camerawork, depth of field photography, and detailed attention to mise-en-scène manifest a distinct approach to cinematic realism, one that Bruns argues aligns with Andre Bazin's ideas about time and space. "Bazin would always insist that the unity of the filmic event be preserved, but it is perhaps truer to say that he insisted on simultaneity without unity – for a single shot sustained, without cutting, would inevitably have multiple centers of gravity or, in musical terms, a multiplicity of independent voices, vying, it would seem, for the spectator's attention" (2008, p. 196).

On a fundamental level, even in those moments when the film engages techniques other than deep focus or a long take – such as in its frenetic editing or standard framing – it is styled and structured in terms of "multiple centers." This goes beyond a mere democratic approach to characters by placing the director on an equal footing with the protagonists. Bruns remarks, "Polyphony presupposes that the *author* become not just a *speaker*, but a *listener* as well" (original italics) (2008, p. 199). Comparing Anderson to the novelist Fyodor Dostoevsky, he suggests that the director "engages with his characters as equals; that is, as other subjects" (2008, p. 199). This perspective supports the notion that the director is not positioning himself as an

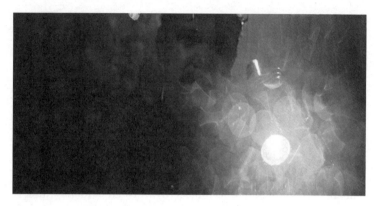

Kurring searches for answers

authority who presides "over" the characters. The camera sometimes seemingly aligns with an omniscient perspective, it is true.
Yet, this apparent position of authority is neither more powerful
nor more all-knowing than any of the characters, or than
Anderson himself.

Consider for example a significant shot that captures a
moment of vulnerable questioning for Jim Kurring. It occurs at
the two-hour mark as a culminating point for a sequence chapter
titled "meltdowns." Each of the protagonists has hit a breaking
point as the camera cuts to Jim in frontal close up. Rainsoaked in
the twilight, he stands in a downpour looking toward the ground,
pointing his illuminated flashlight downward. He is searching
for his gun, which he has recklessly lost, in hopes of retrieving it
before his police squadron arrives to look for it. For Jim, this is
the ultimate in humiliation, given that he prides himself on
"doing the job right" and keeping the community safe. With
tears rolling down his face, he calls out, "Oh Lord, why is this
happening to me? God please help me figure this out; I'm lost
out here. I don't understand why this is happening God." As
sirens sound in the background, indicating the approach of the

police, he slowly lifts his head and looks toward the camera. In an explicit occasion of direct address, he confronts both the spectator and the implied director while also appearing to look towards a higher power for meaning and direction. He gradually tilts the flashlight upward, in the direction of the camera, until the glare of the torch's bulb almost fully envelops the frame. As he continues to stare into the lens, with the sound of ensuing police sirens, a proverbial white light practically blinds us until a cut finally moves to a shot of Claudia (also in tears).

In this state of sheer vulnerability, Jim looks to us, to Anderson, and to God for a solution ("please help me figure this out") but also for an answer ("why is this happening?"). The film's ambiguity and open-endedness – and its polyphony – finds confirmation here, as each potential subject (including the seemingly most powerful, God) appears to be at a loss. However, *Magnolia* finds it most important to simply stand alongside the character, rather than to react with authority or superiority. Again, the point – the "answer," so to speak – is to bear witness to the experience. About the film in general, Bruns posits, "We cannot, as it were, turn away from the character. It's as if Anderson were saying to us, 'don't look at me, I don't know either'" (2008, p. 207). Jim's moment of loss offers a consummate example in which Anderson replies with bewilderment, humility and compassion. The God-subject envisioned by the film responds in the same way.

The film's polyphonic status has implications for the politics of gender and race. Bruns explains how polyphony relates to social consciousness, proposing: "Rather than annex large chunks of narrative space for their own purposes, [polyphonic texts] transform the narrative into an ethical space that forces major characters to experience what Emmanuel Levinas calls 'proximity'" (2008, p. 202). Hence, *Magnolia* constructs a narrative in which personal choices embody ideologically significant acts. Just as we are placed close to Jim as he confronts the camera doubtfully, the characters are pulled into proximity as they navigate a larger moral and social order. For Bruns (drawing on Levinas), such mandatory closeness poses questions of responsibility and obligation (2008, p. 202). The characters learn a sense of responsibility for each other and for the socio-political world they inhabit.

The scenes with Dixon (the African-American boy who wants to help Kurring solve the murder) offer great insight into the way that polyphony creates an ethical space. Tied to a storyline with Marcie and the Worm – in ways that the viewers cannot fully understand (unless we piece them together through the published screenplay and other supporting materials) – Dixon knows who killed the victim discovered by Jim in Marcie's apartment. It turns out that Marcie, his grandmother, strangled the man, who is his grandfather, in order to end the man's abuse of her grandson and son (Worm). In a deleted scene from the script, Marcie reveals to the police, "I killed my husband. He hit my son and then he hit my grandson and I hit him [...] I strangled my husband to protect my boys" (Anderson, 2000, p. 192). This is a fact left ambiguous in the final cut. As Dixon follows Jim to his patrol car, he tries to disclose this crucial information, which carries symbolic implications given that this son would be confessing the crimes of both his mother and his father. While Dixon's main appearance is limited to this interaction with Jim – in which he performs a rap song that holds integral clues to the case – his narrative and thematic role carries great value. In other words, though he appears to be a marginal voice, Dixon holds every bit as much import as the implied protagonists.

In this scene, which takes place in the street outside Marcie's apartment, Dixon walks alongside Jim. The boy appeals, "Tell me what you know; I'll tell you what I know [...] I can help you solve the case." Kurring does not take him seriously. As their dialogue ensues,

A subjective shot from Dixon's point of view

Dixon continually positions himself in an equivalent and reciprocal position of knowledge with the adult figure of authority. He persists when he sees that the latter tries to brush him off, as he repeatedly reasserts the relevance of his own voice. One of Kurring's primary character weaknesses is revealed here; he neglects to see (and hear) the true weight of Dixon's worth. He does not merely miss out on a clue in the case; he forfeits an opportunity to engage in an established and unfolding ethical space.

Jim pauses long enough to listen to Dixon's rap song in which the latter says, "Check that ego – Come off it./I'm the profit – the professor./I'ma teach you 'bout the Worm,/who eventually turned to catch wreck," and ends with a forecast that "the Good Lord [will] bring the rain in." Mid-way through, Dixon declares, "Shut the fuck up, try to listen and learn." Jim's knee-jerk reaction to the child's vulgar language prevents him from tuning in so that he can "listen and learn." In a distinctive wide angle, over-the-shoulder shot from Dixon's point of view, we see Jim through Dixon's eyes. This static and fixed frame, which follows the fast-pace action surrounding the rap, captures the futility that Dixon feels. The heavy subjective camerawork conveys just how clearly he is being dismissed. As the shot remains inside his point of view, he runs down the street, chasing after Jim as he drives away. Dixon calls out, "I told you who did it and you're not even listening to me."

As one of the film's many centers, Dixon's subjectivity takes on crucial importance. As Bruns puts it, "A minor character in *Magnolia* does not shift our attention away from a central character […] *every* character seems to participate as a minor character" (original italics) (2008, p. 203). What Dixon lacks in screen time, he makes up for in symbolic import. A case might even be made that his perceived marginality actually works in a way that centralizes and prioritizes him, because his limited presence in fact highlights the silences and gaps in the diegesis. In addition, Dixon is privileged by virtue of the fact that he is a young boy within a larger narrative economy that values childhood (especially boyhood) over almost any other circumstance. He, like Stanley, knows more than the adults and is more sympathetic than most of the other characters simply because he is dismissed and devalued. In the published screenplay, Dixon and Stanley cross paths several times in a diner. The former is sitting across the table from his father, Worm, when they spot the latter, whom they recognize as the quiz show kid. Through exchanged glances, they form a plan for Worm to play on Stanley's sympathies in order to take his money. These scenes end in a confrontation where Dixon holds a gun on Stanley – demanding cash – while Worm convinces his son that violence is not the way.

The Dixon-Worm-Stanley thread results in a transformation for each character. Dixon finally attains a sense of love and acceptance from his distant father. Stanley achieves a similar sense of fatherly approval from this surrogate. Worm crosses a moral threshold, in choosing not to commit the robbery, which suggests he may have gained a renewed ethical perspective. These missing parts also explain other gaps, such as the reason that Jim's gun "miraculously" falls from the sky. (Dixon has thrown it out of a moving car window.) Though, again, to assess its narrative value may be to miss the point. The mostly invisible story thread registers as an overarching, influential pressure on the film – a symbolic fragment that asserts the worth of Dixon's voice in a world that looks determined to silence it.

Chapter 5

Redemption and Re-Mediation
Framing the Deathbed

Magnolia's use of multiple narrative voices – its polyphonic approach – helps to define it as millennial cinema. The characters and storylines organize into a series of overlapping concentric circles. This de-centered structure is symptomatic of the fact that the film addresses a historical transition. Bidding goodbye to one era and ushering in the next, *Magnolia* resists binary oppositions and instead incorporates circular shapes and cyclical patterns. In the opening title sequence, the flower blossom, with its round shape and ever-expanding movement signals the film's governing principles of circularity. Much of the film's camerawork accentuates rotating pans and dolly shots as well as whip pans that turn out of one scene into the next. In addition, the bookend device of the narrative voice-over returns at the conclusion, in cyclical fashion, to explore the initial questions of coincidence and chance.

Through its circularity, *Magnolia* articulates a preoccupation with the millennium. It is deeply rooted in its historical moment, absorbed by the ideological concerns of the late 1990s. Yet, temporally, the film lives simultaneously in the past, present, and future, continually doubling back toward the end of the nineteenth century before motioning toward an unknown twenty-first century

Magnolia, by Christina Lane   © Christina Lane. Published by John Wiley & Sons Ltd

future. While situated within the forward-looking cycle of crisis films, *Magnolia* romances the fin de siècle – a time of the inception of cinema and the dawn of modernity.

A circular pattern also appears in the phrase, "We may be through with the past but the past ain't through with us," which is spoken three times in the film.[1] Derived from a quotation by professor and television personality Bergan Evans (in the 1946 anti-superstition book *The Natural History of Nonsense*), the maxim invokes a cyclical view of time through its very wording. For these characters, it is not a matter of living "in" the past or present, but living the past "through" the present. Moreover, as part of the millennial thread of *Magnolia*, this line affirms the importance and inescapability of the past. In the climactic frog sequence, (most of) the characters arrive at "the end of the world as they know it." Yet as they head into a new future, it seems important that they bring the past with them. Like the "male epiphany films" discussed in Chapter 1, the characters have awakened to a fresh perspective on prior events. They have been re-born to new possibilities, achieving a chance to fashion an altered identity.

As we have seen in previous chapters, the past is bound up in questions about the future of paternal authority, technology, and the media. When *Magnolia* contemplates the shift from century to century (whether occurring in the 1890s or the 1990s) or from millennium to millennium, it channels these questions of time and history into father-son relationships and corollary concerns of industry and communication. Put another way, *Magnolia* stages centennial and millennial shifts in terms of intergenerational conflicts. Paternal-filial relationships stand in for broader points of crisis regarding the past, present, and future. They also mediate tensions between film, television, and digitality, as indicated by the film's numerous references to silent cinema, television, and various Hollywood forefathers as well as its use of computer generated effects. *Magnolia* circles around these crisis points in an effort to resolve questions of male power and technology, yet part of its continual looping stems from the fact that the film seeks to transform the future while being limited to the tools of the present. It is concerned with the media of patriarchy, so to speak.

Magnolia does not reconcile the conflicts between fathers and sons, or between film, television, and emerging technologies. Instead these themes are held in tension, further contributing to the play of contradiction. The film appears to be suspended in time, inhabiting several temporal spaces at once and leaving the father–son relationship unresolved. An array of stylistic devices keeps the focus on thematic and narrative "in-between" spaces, searching out the ambiguities that make resolution difficult.

This closing chapter examines the notion that *Magnolia* attempts to reinvent cinematic language even as, and perhaps because, it appears oppressed by the existing vocabulary of film. If apocalyptic cinema typically involves a re-awakening of its characters, then here we find an effort to re-awaken the medium of film. Embedded in its investigation of redemption rests a broader struggle to redeem cinema by "re-mediating" it through existing and emerging forms of technology. Various objects and techniques, such as the Pathé camera, the telestrator, the recurring appearances of television sets, and even the extensive Anderson-designed, promotional website, gather in and around *Magnolia*. They cross the apparent borders between film, television, digitality, and the Internet while also stretching boundaries of time and space (moving from 1911 Greenberry Hill, Connecticut to the 1999 San Fernando Valley).

The film's interest in the future life of cinema relates directly to the deathbed that takes center stage. Earl, the dying patriarch, embodies all of these contradictions; he represents both the history of television (as an industry executive) and the history of film (in that he is played by Robards, who had an extensive film as well as television background). It is also notable that the introduction to Earl brings together a kaleidoscope of forms, including animation, industrial films, and digital effects, when the camera "enters" his body and "envisions" his lung cancer. An intersection occurs, centered almost literally within Earl, where all of these representational forms come together and where the life of the father figure is at stake. This is one reason that his speech about regret, an eight-minute monologue that occurs in the film's second half, carries such power. As Earl lists his regrets to his caretaker Phil, we gain a glimpse into his personal perspective; we experience one version of paternal subjectivity. He is obviously troubled by his own legacy as well as that of male dominance in general. He hovers between life and death, articulating his sorrow and self-disgust and fundamentally critiquing his own misogynistic ways.

Earl's monologue is distinctive, emphasizing transformation and reinvention. He may be dying but he leaves in his wake various possibilities for masculine identity, which are embodied in the remaining male characters. While the film makes clear that there is no escape from the legacy of patriarchy, possibilities exist within *Magnolia* for challenging the hold of traditional male authority through some of the very terms that govern its representation – using the language of film and media. The high voltage energy of *Magnolia* – which some reviewers identify as its audacity or nerve – signifies this urge to free up the medium. The desire to "break out of confinement," as described by Diane Sippl, is further expressed by the open narrative field. Therefore, the spatial tension between claustrophobia and freedom plays a crucial role as a meta-cinematic device. *Magnolia* implies that the medium is at an impasse, a crisis that problematizes the past and grasps toward the future.

The Power of Regret

Earl's deathbed speech provides an illustration of *Magnolia*'s ever-shifting perspective. Earl speaks to Phil, though he speaks about Frank. That is, he addresses a son-surrogate in his efforts to connect with his biological son. Phil and Frank triangulate around Earl, embodying two son-figures who play contradictory roles in Earl's narrative. Phil represents vulnerability, nurturing, and earnestness; Frank embodies defensiveness, anger, and self-deception. The proponent of "Seduce and Destroy" may display a deep-seated hatred of women but his extreme misogyny acts as a cover for his even deeper hostility toward Earl for abandoning him (Bruzzi, 2008). In fact, as Frank's story emerges, it is clear that he identifies with his mother and loathes his father (a situation that mirrors Cruise's own biography). Phil therefore functions as a mediator for the father-son relationship, with the ultimate goal of healing the past. He takes on the role of witness discussed in Chapter 4, whereby he validates and experiences the emotions felt by Frank and Earl. Like Mann, he plays a choral part, enunciating the affective dimensions of the father-son relationship. Also like Mann, he models a certain degree of accountability, taking responsibility for his actions and emotions. Therefore, as a mediator, an enunciator, and a listener, Phil offers alternative responses to the tensions represented by Earl and Frank.

Earl begins his monologue by explaining to Phil, "I'm gonna try to talk and I'm gonna try to say something." As his speech, which is at times incoherent and delirious, continues, he proceeds to describe his love affair with his first wife, Lilly, who was Frank's mother. Though he felt deeply for her, he was a philanderer and adulterer, looking to assert his "manliness." He assumes full blame for his womanizing, recognizing that his actions diminished her freedom and agency. The effect of Earl's self-indictment is to strip bare the structures of patriarchy, exposing an underlying destructive logic. He regrets that his idea of manhood had extremely negative consequences for his wife. He laments losing his wife and child by both driving them away and abandoning them. He declares, "This is the regret that you make."

The camera initially curves around the room, establishing a relational space between Earl and Phil. Then, after a series of close ups and medium shots on Earl, with occasional reverse shots on Phil, the film cuts away from Earl's room. As the dying man continues to speak, a series of edits moves from character to character in separate spaces and co-existing scenes. We see Gator's wife and assistant ushering him from the car to his home in the rain; Claudia taking a shower and preparing to snort cocaine; a group of policemen scouring a riverbank as they search for Kurring's gun; Donnie preparing to rob the safe; Linda downing an overdose of pills; Stanley reading a host of library books; and Frank sitting in his car as he considers knocking on his father's door.

The sound of these scenes is muted, at times imperceptible and at others completely silent. Aside from Earl's voice, only various forms of water can be heard, such as the rain outside of Gator's house, Claudia's shower stream, or the downpour along the river where Jimmy searches for his gun. The water serves as a preface for the ensuing cathartic downpour (and "Wise Up" song) that is about to reach across the cinematic span of all the characters. The variations of water therefore accentuate the spatial connectedness between them, reinforcing the relational cinematography and editing.

Earl's words reverberate as though in an echo chamber, eerily punctuating his inescapable grief and remorse. His monologue comes to a close as he makes a counter-argument against the impulse – often expressed in male melodramas – to resolve or come to terms with one's wrongs. He suggests, "Don't let anyone

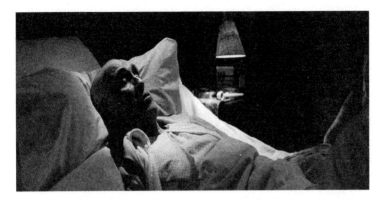

Earl's deathbed

say to you, 'You shouldn't regret anything' [...] You regret what
you fucking want. Use that regret." This speech burrows down
deep into the emotional consequences of abusive power. It offers
few "outs" – no excuses or solutions. Claustrophobic and confining, especially in terms of sound, the sequence gestures
toward the seeming inescapability of patriarchal power. Through
its melodramatic tone, the monologue strikes at the affective
core of male dominance, asserting that the ideological implications of individual actions cannot be ignored, downplayed, or
wished away.

According to Earl, regret becomes a motivating factor for
personal and institutional change. As his words wind down, he says
in a self-aware and referential way, "That's a long way to go with no
punch." He knows that he is playing out a role in a patriarch's
deathbed scene. Perhaps even more significantly, he hits a wall.
There is no conclusion – "no punch" – because the film does not
necessarily see a way forward. The only solution provided by Earl
is to remain suspended in the evident, irresolvable contradictions.
Use the regret; don't lose it. In other words, Earl suggests, remain
vulnerable to your emotions.

This sequence provides yet another instance of the "theater of vulnerability," in which emotional strength and weakness stand in for broader ideological concerns of power. Earl opens up, dropping any pretense of authority and advocating for overall humility. Phil too plays a vulnerable role as witness to Earl's story and, later, when Frank pleads for his father to stay alive. Like Mann's music, Phil supports the position that there is strength in weakness. He attempts to create an ethical and honest space for an emotional exchange between father and son.

Furthermore, Earl and Phil both experience a form of "minorness" as described by Bruns. They come out of their comfort zones and confront their own weaknesses. Earl does so by letting down his guard and engaging with his own painful memories. Phil does so simply by listening to Earl's story, making himself available to raw self-expression. The television executive wrestles with his own efforts to commandeer power over those he has loved. The nurse comes to terms with the fact that he may not be able to heal this particular wound. They do not attempt to be heroic; they recognize their smallness in the world.

Frank will achieve this sense of minorness when he enters Earl's space. His initial anger transmutes into pain, as he begs for his father not to die. For all of his posturing of power and dominance through most of the film, he finally experiences utter powerlessness. After sobbing uncontrollably, he gazes into Earl's eyes as the latter takes his final breath. Here, Frank is positioned in close proximity to his father, which is emphasized by the camera's lens. Within *Magnolia*'s terms, closeness equals minorness. Frank drops his guard, unable to grandstand in his usual way. He is humbled by Earl's death.

The value placed on humility and vulnerability in this film – its representation of its characters as well as its spectators as

Stanley stares at the rain of frogs with wonder

"minor" – may have played a solid role in the ambivalence expressed by reviewers. For this reason, it was labeled "embarrassingly sincere" as well as "audacious and excruciating" (Udovitch, 2000, p. 50; Hirschberg, 1999, p. 52). For all of its high style, *Magnolia* is distinctly raw. This rawness comes from the fact that it pushes up against the edges of existing cinematic codes. Not afraid to stumble or expose itself, *Magnolia* issues a summons to re-enliven cinema with all of the available tools of the past and the quickly moving present. Just as the patriarchal figure of Earl seeks redemption from his son, the film looks to redeem the medium. At the same instance that the son finds himself vulnerable at the moment of his father's death, the film appears vulnerable too – perhaps exposed to the future. In this way, *Magnolia* is both epical and epochal. Romney proposes that it is "one film at the millennium that suggests cinema still does mean something" (2000, p. 77). *Magnolia* is both pre- and post-cinematic, apparently haunted by, yet inspired by, the past as well as the future.

The last section of the film, in which the voice-over narration returns and we see each character's final scene, *feels* like a re-awakening. Through slow motion and slow-moving figures on screen, the characters appear to "come to." They surface to a new reality. Many of them are lying down (Earl on a stretcher, Frank on a sofa, Linda on a hospital gurney, Claudia in her bed), as though awaking from a dream. The narrator states, "There are stories of coincidence and chance and intersections and strange things told. We generally say, 'Well, if that was in a movie, I wouldn't believe it.'" Using irony, the film reflects on reality, suggesting that at times real life seems to be filled with movie-ish contrivances and because of this, conversely, we should perhaps believe in *Magnolia's* synchronicity.

This occurs at another point, previously mentioned, during the rain of frogs. In Claudia's apartment, the camera tracks upward and slowly focuses on an out of place string of words seemingly pasted onto a painting. "But it really did happen," the sign reads, reminding some audience members and signaling to others that there have been documented cases of such rain (as well as the account in Exodus 8:2). Such a moment encourages us to cross over the line from skepticism to open-mindedness – to drop any sense of judgment and "believe" in the movie. It not only pushes at the boundaries of cinema (by breaking the fourth wall if nothing else), but it also pushes at the edges of reality. The close up on the sign of the wall is followed by a short scene with Stanley in which he watches the rain with wonder and says, with awe, "This happens. This is something that happens." By watching the transformation occur in the real world outside the window, he too is transformed. His notions of what is possible have completely shifted. Anderson appears to be asking his audience to change our sense of the possible – on screen – as well.

As an instance of millennial film, *Magnolia* asks its audience to "believe" in cinema even while challenging us to imagine new codes and conventions through more recent technology. However, it goes further, relating these questions of belief to the concerns of its historical moment – most specifically the material excesses of the 1990s. *Magnolia* invites us into a conversation about ethical choices related to the everyday. It attempts to see the possibilities of film anew, reminding us in the process of the ethical dimensions of the medium.

Notes

Introduction

1   See Geoff King's *Donnie Darko* (2007), which explores director Richard Kelly's rise to cult status.

Chapter 1: *Magnolia* at the Millennium

1   The rain of frogs alludes to references other than Exodus 8:2 and, in fact, Anderson has said that he was not fully aware of this scripture when he conceived of the "plague." One source of inspiration was early twentieth-century writer Charles Fort, who studied many unexplained natural phenomena including "falling frogs." A second source comes from ancient Rome, when the health of a society was judged by its frogs (See Anderson, 2000, pp. 206–7).

2   For more on the Exodus passage in relation to *Magnolia*, see DeGiglio-Bellemare, (2000).

3   Regarding Y2K, the use of two-digit codes (the last two digits) in the representation of years, as units, created potential problems for the changeover from 1999 to 2000.

4   *Office Space* might also be placed in the "male epiphany" cycle, given its emphasis on the mechanization and de-humanization of the

Magnolia, by Christina Lane   © Christina Lane. Published by John Wiley & Sons Ltd

workplace. While not a drama, thriller, or science fiction film, *Office Space* was released in 1999 and suggests that millennial cinema includes comedy.

Chapter 2: Through the Viewfinder of a Cinematic "Son"

1 It is also the case that many of the "cool," male directors foster complicated and/or sympathetic female characters upon close examination of their films. In this respect, a consideration of Anderson helps us to see the work of these filmmakers in a different light. Coolness is only one dimension (among many) of their personas.

2 In another instance of intertextuality, Julianne Moore's performance of Linda draws on her prior characterization of the melodramatic figure of Carol White in Todd Haynes' *Safe* (1995). The tensions between emotional surface and depth that define these two characters would continue in *The Hours* (2002), *Far From Heaven* (2003), and *The Prizewinner of Defiance, Ohio* (2007).

Chapter 3: An Aesthetics of Contradiction

1 For more on the "infinitely expanding middle" and on "television as melodrama" in general, see Lynne Joyrich (1988).

2 Since the latter film is obviously influenced by the former, it is particularly noteworthy that women fare far better in *Magnolia*. Perhaps as much a function of *Network*'s historical moment than any particular decisions by Lumet or Anderson, the female protagonist Diane Christensen (Faye Dunaway) comes off as a shrill, cold and ultimately irredeemable figure. Wholly a product of the corporate structure and willing to exploit any political position, she represents a grotesque image of an independent working woman at the height of the second-wave feminist movement. *Magnolia* operates as a corrective to *Network*'s politics by presenting sympathetic female characters.

Chapter 4: Sound and Voice

1   "Deathly" is not in the film but on the soundtrack. "One" was originally
     performed by Three Dog Night.

Chapter 5: Redemption and Re-Mediation

1   This line is said separately by Jimmy Gator, Donnie Smith, and the narrator.

Bibliography

Anderson, P.T. 2000. *Magnolia: The Shooting Script*. New York: Newmarket Press.

Bartlett, T. 2005. "Hit Mann." *salon*, available at www.salon.com/entertainment/feature/2005/04/04/aimee_mann (accessed September 3, 2010).

Bazin, A. 1967. "The Evolution of the Language of Cinema." *What is Cinema, Vol. 1* (trans. Hugh Gray), Berkeley and Los Angeles: University of California Press, pp. 23–40.

Benson, S. 2003. "For Want of a Better Term?: Polyphony and the Value of Music in Bakhtin and Kundera." *Narrative*, 11.3 (October): 292–311.

Bessman, J. 1999. "Mann Blossoms on Reprise Soundtrack." *Billboard*, 111, November 13, p. 46.

Bordwell, D. 1985. *Narration in the Fiction Film*. Madison: University of Wisconsin Press.

Bordwell, D., Staiger, J., and Thompson, K. 1988. *The Classical Hollywood Cinema: Film Style and Mode of Production to 1960*. London and New York: Routledge.

Borrelli, C. 2000. "Lights! Camera! Action!." *Toledo Blade*, available at http://toledoblade.com (accessed August 10, 2009).

Bruns, J. 2008. "The polyphonic film." *New Review of Film and Television Studies*, 6.2 (August): 189–212.

Bruzzi, S. 2008. *Bringing Up Daddy: Fatherhood and Masculinity in Postwar Hollywood*. London: British Film Institute.

Cowie, P. 1982. *Ingmar Bergman: A Critical Biography*. New York: Scribners.

DeGiglio-Bellemare, M. 2000. "*Magnolia* and the Sign of the Times: A Theological Reflection." *Journal of Religion and Film*, www.unomaha.edu/jrf/magnolia.htm (accessed September 6, 2010).

Denby, D. 1999. "San Fernando Aria." *New Yorker*, 75.39 (December 20): 102–4.

Dienst, R. 1994. *Still Life in Real Time: Theory after Television*. Durham, NC: Duke University Press.

Dillman, J.C. 2005. "Twelve Characters in Search of a Televisual Text: *Magnolia* Masquerading as Soap Opera." *Journal of Popular Film and Television*, 33.3 (Fall): 143–50.

Evans, B. 1946. *The Natural History of Nonsense*. New York: A.A. Knopf.

Feit, J.S. 2004. "Sacred Symbols and the Depiction of Religions in Millennial Movies, 1997–2002." *Journal of Media and Religion*, 3.3 (August): 133–50.

Ferguson, O.W. 1959. "Swift's Saeva Indignatio and A Modest Proposal." *Philological Quarterly*, 38.4 (October): 473–9.

Fischer, L. 2008. "Theory into Practice: En-gendering Narrative in *Magnolia*." In *Screening Genders* (eds. K. Gabbard and W. Luhr), New Brunswick, NJ: Rutgers University Press, pp. 29–48

Fiske, J. 1988. *Television Culture*. London and NY: Routledge.

Fraiman, S. 2003. *Cool Men and the Second Sex*. New York: Columbia University Press.

Fuchs, C. nd. "TV Land." *PopMatters*. www.popmatters.com/film/reviews/m/magnolia2.shtml (accessed September 6, 2010).

Hamad, H. 2008. "Postfeminist Fatherhood and Contemporary Hollywood Stardom." PhD dissertation, University of East Anglia.

Hipps, S. 2003. "The Exodus for Kids." *Metaphilm*, available at http://metaphilm.com/index.php/detail/magnolia/ (accessed September 3, 2010).

Hirschberg, L. 1999. "His Way." *New York Times Magazine*, December 19: 52–6.

Hudak, D. 2004. "Don't You Like Me: The Films of Paul Thomas Anderson." Master's thesis, University of Miami Coral Gables, FL.

Hunter, J. 2000. "It's a Mann's Mann's World." *Village Voice*, February 15: 109, 115.

Jacobson, M.F., and González, G. 2006. *What Have They Built You to Do?: The Manchurian Candidate and Cold War America*. Minneapolis: University of Minnesota Press.

Joyrich, L. 1988. "All That Television Allows: TV Melodrama, Postmodernism, and Consumer Culture." *Camera Obscura*, 16: 129–53.

King, G. 2007. *Donnie Darko*. New York and London: Wallflower Press.

Klawans, S. 2000. "Films." *Nation*, February 7: 34–6.

Kleinhans, C. 1998. "Independent Features: Hopes and Dreams." *The New American Cinema* (ed. Jon Lewis), Durham, NC: Duke University Press, pp. 307–27.

Kuntzel, T. 1980. "The Film-Work, 2." *Camera Obscura* (Spring): 7–68.

Lamm, R. 1991. "Can We Laugh at God?" *Journal of Film and Television*, 19.2 (Summer): 81–90.

Marks, L. 2000. *The Skin of the Film: Intercultural Cinema, Embodiment, and the Senses*. Durham, NC: Duke University Press.

Maslin, J. 1999. "Entangled Lives on the Cusp of the Millennium." *The New York Times*, December 17: E15.

McCullough, J. 2000. Book Review: "Apocalypse Movies: End of the World Cinema." *Cineaction*, 53 (November): 53–5.

Merritt, A.T. (1939) *Sixteenth Century Plainsong: A Basic for the Study of Counterpoint*. Cambridge, MA. Harvard University Press.

Mottram, J. 2006. *The Sundance Kids: How the Mavericks Took Back Hollywood*. New York, Macmillan.

Olsen, M. 2000. "Singing in the Rain." *Sight and Sound*, 10.3 (March): 26–30.

Reay, P. 2008. *Music in Film: Soundtracks and Synergy*. London and New York, Wallflower Press.

Rogin, M. 1987. *Ronald Reagan the Movie, and Other Episodes in Political Demonology*. Berkeley and Los Angeles: University of California Press.

Romney, J. 2000. "Every Petal Tells a Story." *New Statesman*, March 20: 45–6.

Sconce, J. (2002) "Irony, Nihilism, and the New American 'Smart' Film." *Screen*, 43.4 (Winter): 349–69.

Silverstone, R. 1994. *Television and Everyday Life*. London and New York: Routledge.

Sippl, D. (2000) "Tomorrow is My Birthday: Placing Apocalypse in Millennial Cinema." *Cineaction*, 53, November: 2–21.

Tripp, D. 2005. "Wake Up!: Narratives of Masculine Epiphany." *Quarterly Review of Film and Video*, 22: 181–8.

Turan, K. (1999). "*Magnolia*: Random Lives, Bound By Chance." *Los Angeles Times*, www.calendarlive.com/movies/reviews/cl-movie000406-90,0,1163360.story (accessed September 6, 2010).

Udovitch, M. 2000. "The Epic Obsessions of Paul Thomas Anderson." *Rolling Stone*, February 3: 46–9, 69.

Waxman, S. 2005. *Rebels on the Backlot: Six Maverick Directors and How They Conquered the Hollywood System*. New York: Harper.

Williams, R. 1974. *Television, Technology, and Cultural Form*. London: Fontana.

Willman, C. 2000. "Mann Crazy." *Entertainment Weekly*, January 7: 67.

Wollen, P. 1986. "Godard and Counter Cinema: Vent d'est." In *Narrative Apparatus Ideology: A Film Theory Reader* (ed. P. Rosen), New York: Columbia University Press, pp. 120–9.

Index

affect 6, 39–40, 99
 dampened 40
 gender 81, 101
 in *Magnolia* 26, 39
 and melodrama 26
 and music 79–80, 81–2, 83
 and "smart cinema" 39–40, 45
 standing in for social/political
  concerns 26–7
Altman, Robert 38, 47–8, 50, 56
American Beauty (2000) 31, 34
Anderson, Ernie 50, 56
Anderson, Paul Thomas 2, 21,
 37–57, 70, 87–9
 and Altman 47–8
 career 37–9
 and father–son
  relationship 38–9, 46, 50,
  51, 56, 57
 and gender 56, 57
 Magnolia website 43, 97
 music 33, 80–2, 84–5

and New Line Studio 37
and other filmmakers 38–9, 47
and Robards 49–50
and Scorsese 49
and "smart cinema" 46
 techniques 41, 87–8
animation 67–8, 98
 see also technology
apocalyptic cinema 27–9, 97
 see also millennial cinema
authorship 21–2, 87–9
 and 1970s directors 38–9, 47
 and 1990s directors 7, 38
 and address 47
 and affect 39–40
 and extra-cinematic
  materials 9
 and father–son themes 7–8,
  38–9, 47–9
 and intertextuality 47–9
 and masculinity 38, 81
 and multiplicity 8–9, 82–3

authorship (cont'd)
  and music 81–3
  and polyphony 8–9, 82–3,
    87–9
  and "smart cinema" 40–1
  and trope of "cool"
    director 38–9

Babel (2000) 6
Bazin, Andre 48, 87
Blackman, Jeremy 4
Boogie Nights (1997) 6
Bordwell, David 41–2, 75
Bruns, John 80, 82, 86–90, 92,
  102

cancer 46, 50
capitalism 24–6, 31, 33, 76
closure, lack of 73–5, 92
Cold War era 27–9
COPS 33, 69–70
Crash (2004) 22
Cruise, Tom 4, 51–6

Demme, Jonathan 47, 49, 51
digitality 9, 96, 98
  see also technology
Dillman, Joanne Clarke
  71–4, 81

Evans, Bergan 96

Feit, Jonathan Scott 23, 30
Fight Club (1999) 29, 31, 34
fin de siècle 9, 34, 96

Fraiman, Susan 38–40
Fuchs, Cynthia 69, 71

Generation X 25
gender 31–4, 89–90
  and affect 99
  and American Beauty 31–4
  and authorship 81–2
  and contradiction 34, 101
  and ethics 89–90
  and Fight Club 31–4
  and intergenerational
    conflicts 96–102
  masculinity studies 8
  and The Matrix 31–4
  and millennial cinema 29–35,
    96–8
  and "minorness" 102
  and music 81–2
  and polyphony 89–90
  and race 89–90
  and Signs 31–4
  and technology 96–8
  and themes of
    awakening 31–2, 35, 96–8
  see also masculinity
genre 27, 79
Gibson, Henry 50
Grace, April 4

Hall, Philip Baker 3, 48, 50
Hammad, Hannah 51–2
Hard Eight (1996) 39
Hill Street Blues 69
Hipps, Shane 19, 35

independent cinema 38–9, 41–2
Internet 8, 42–3, 96–7
intertextuality 42, 47, 50
    see also reflexivity
irony 55–6, 104

Jay, Ricky 2, 11, 15, 82

King, Cleo 3
Kiss Me Deadly (1955) 28–9
knowingness 54, 90–3, 104
Kuntzel, Thierry 11

Los Angeles 22, 81–2
Lumet, Sidney 38, 47, 49, 76

Macy, William H. 4
Magnolia (1999)
    "awakening," themes of 28,
        31–3, 97–104
    awards 2
    chance vs. grand design 15,
        104
    childhood in 14, 32, 92, 104
    cinematography 48, 49, 59–60,
        62–9, 87–9, 91–2, 95, 100
    deathbed 97, 99–102
    editing in 60–71, 73, 87, 100
    ethics and morality in 43–4,
        80, 89–90, 92, 101, 105
    Exodus 8:2 6, 19–20, 104
    fate in 40–5
    fathers and sons, themes of 39,
        46–52, 56–7, 92–3, 98–103
    and film literacy 47

    as independent film 37
    and "inexpressibility" 61–2
    inter-generational conflicts
        in 39, 47–51, 96–102
    as musical 79–80
    opening sequence 11–15
    and orphanhood 56
    power relations in 83, 85, 87,
        100–1
    rain of frogs 6, 17–20, 26, 35,
        42–3, 96, 104
    redemption in 97–104
    regret in 98–101
    weather reports 20–1, 35
"male epiphany films" 31–4, 96
Mann, Aimee 2, 33, 79–86, 99,
    102
    authorship 8
    collaboration with
        Anderson 80–2
    and flow 69
    and multiplicity 8, 79
    "One" song 61–2
    and polyphony 8, 80
    "Save Me" video 86
    struggles with producers
        83–4
    and 'Til Tuesday 84
    as unifying presence 79, 82–6
    "Wise Up" song 33, 82, 84–6
Marks, Laura 62
masculinity 8, 51–7, 96–102
    see also gender
Matrix, The (1999) 31, 34
melodrama 27, 100

Melvin and Howard
    (1980) 49–51
millennial cinema 2, 22–35, 68,
    76, 103–5
    1990s films 23–7
    American Beauty 31–4
    and Cold War cinema 27–9
    and existentialism 22–3
    and father–son
        relationships 96–7
    Fight Club 31–4
    and gender 29–35, 56, 96–8
    The Matrix 31–4
    and polyphony 95
    Signs 31–4
    themes of awakening 22–35,
        96–7
    see also apocalyptic cinema
"minorness" 87, 90–3, 102
mise-en-scène 42, 48, 65, 83, 87
misogyny 44, 51–4, 98, 99, 101
    see also gender
Moore, Julianne 4
multiplicity 8, 61, 71–7, 79–93,
    95
music 48, 79–87
    see also polyphony

Network (1976) 76–7
New Line Cinema 37

polyphony 8, 80, 86–7, 89–90, 95
    see also authorship
proximity 59–60, 80, 88–90, 102
Pulp Fiction (1994) 13

race, ideologies of 89–93
reflexivity 7, 42, 45–6, 51, 55,
    101, 104
    see also intertextuality
Reilly, John C. 3
Ridgely, Robert 50
Robards, Jason 4, 49–50, 56
Romney, Jonathan 46, 104

"Save Me" music video 83
Sconce, Jeffrey 6–7, 39–43
Scorsese, Martin 38, 47, 49
"Seduce and Destroy"
    program 52–3, 99
Short Cuts (1993) 6
Signs (2002) 29–30
Sippl, Diane 1, 14, 26–9, 98
slacker 25–6
"smart cinema" 6–7, 39–41, 43,
    45–6, 84
synchronicity 43–4, 104

Tarantino, Quentin 7, 13, 37
technology 54–5, 96–8
telestrator 13, 97
television 9, 50, 55, 60–1, 63–76,
    96–8
    "dailiness" 71, 85
    "flow" 65–6
    seriality 71–4, 82
televisuality 9, 70–2
theater 68
Them! (1954) 27
There Will Be Blood (2007)
    39, 48

'Til Tuesday 84
The Today Show 69
Traffic (2000) 22, 23
Tripp, Daniel 31, 33–4

voice-over 2, 11–15, 82, 95,
    103–4

Walters, Melora 3
What Do Kids Know? show 3–4,
    20, 64, 66–7
"Wise Up" song 34, 84–6
Wollen, Peter 75

Y2K (Year 2000) 23–4